Reudene E. Wilburn

Understanding
the Preschooler

PETER LANG
New York • Washington, D.C./Baltimore • Boston • Bern
Frankfurt am Main • Berlin • Brussels • Vienna • Oxford

Library of Congress Cataloging-in-Publication Data

Wilburn, Reudene E.
Understanding the preschooler / Reudene E. Wilburn.
p. cm. — (Rethinking childhood; vol. 9)
Includes bibliographical references and index.
1. Preschool children—Psychology. 2. Social skills in children.
3. Education, Preschool. I. Title. II. Series.
LB1117.W543   372.21—dc21   98-44188
ISBN 0-8204-4058-2
ISSN 1086-7155

Die Deutsche Bibliothek-CIP-Einheitsaufnahme

Wilburn, Reudene E.:
Understanding the preschooler / Reudene E. Wilburn.
—New York; Washington, D.C./Baltimore; Boston; Bern; Frankfurt am
Main; Berlin; Brussels; Vienna; Oxford: Lang.
(Rethinking childhood; Vol. 9)
ISBN 0-8204-4058-2

Cover design by Lisa Dillon

The paper in this book meets the guidelines for permanence and durability
of the Committee on Production Guidelines for Book Longevity
of the Council of Library Resources.

∞

© 2000 Peter Lang Publishing, Inc., New York

Printed in the United States of America.

Table of Contents

Introduction

The stages that a child passes through both physically and intellectually are interesting to observe as well as crucial to understanding the development that leads to maturation. One of the purposes of observation by social scientists is to better understand the behavior of the youngster as he/she learns and then internalizes the standard norms of interactive behavior in society. Parents, family members, and close friends contribute the primary points of reference to the developmental process, which includes cultural mores first, then later, the broader mores of our society. Parents, family members, and close friends accomplish this *culturing* both directly and indirectly. Youngsters are constantly using the people around them as models, whether the people want to be models or not. Generally speaking, if a youngster sees an adult in his/her life performing an act, using certain language, displaying certain attitudes, and so on, the youngster assumes that is the appropriate way to conduct oneself.

Children learn and imitate what they live with and what they are accustomed to seeing, for the most part, in their formative years. Yes, their personality and egocentric nature play a part, but generally, children act and react to situations as they have seen the members of their family act. For example, a 3-year-old will usually take a toy from the shelf in preschool that he/she wants to play with. If another child attempts to take the toy away from him/her, the first child may say, "No, I want it." But will the first child hit or scream at the offending peer as an immediate response to the peer trying to take the toy away? This writer has observed both (a) the rudimentary beginnings of negotiations between 3-year-old preschoolers, and (b) hitting and screaming between other 3-and-4-year-old preschoolers. Another example, "I want it, I had it, stop it. Don't take it away. Go away. Get the red one. Stop it. I had this one." These are negotiation strategies that the preschooler is using to get his classmate to stop taking the toy away. And, "Ahhhhha, oohhoooo, teacher, teacher, Charles hit me!" "Why did you hit Sarah?" " Because she tried to take the truck from me." This example of (b) above is what the hitter displays because he/she hasn't begun to realize that words can work also in interactions with peers.

Arguably, Sarah has learned not to take the truck from Charles. But, is it a good idea for Charles to learn to hit people who take things from him, or hit people who disagree with him? Perhaps he could learn another way to handle those types of situations. How do the parents of negotiators and the parents of hitters respond to their children at *going-home-time?*

There was a difference in the responses of the parents to their children. Generally, the hitters' parents were hurried in their manner and interaction with their children, and they spoke in louder tones than was necessary. Either they put the coat and hat on their child or told the child to "hurry up, we got to go [*sic*]." There did not seem to be any extended conversation occurring, just a few words from the child to the parent about the events of the day. However, the parents of the negotiators generally handled things differently. The negotiators' parents usually spoke to them in softer tones, seemed more relaxed, and engaged in conversation when their child attempted to talk to them about something. There was more of a give-and-take in the going-home ritual from preschool. Parental types seem to have an influence on the attitude that their children have internalized in the way they interact with peers. "Let's talk," may be a part of what is internalized as the natural way to handle adversity. Or, "I'll hit you if you disagree with me."

Social scientists are constantly eager to learn more about the progression from infancy through early childhood into preadolescence, and then adolescence. The purpose of this book is to introduce and discuss some aspects of the process of early childhood socialization and the beginning progressions of internalizing academic experiences. Theory underpins the discussions, the informal experiments conducted by this writer, and the activities offered here. One of those aspects under discussion is positive social interaction among peers. Positive social interactions among young children are ongoing activities that are learned by being involved with one another in close proximity. These interactions include conversations, playing together, working on projects together, negotiating disagreements, sharing a meal together, and all other situations that include other people. As Brewer and Kieff (1997) noted, "Play helps children's emotional development. . . . They have opportunities to play out their fears and gain control of their anxieties, for example" (p. 92).

Preschools, nursery schools, and day-care centers can bring the assembly of young children that provides opportunity daily for ongoing interaction. Minuchin and Shapiro (1983) observed that social competence includes the ability to interact with peers and develop the skill of negotiating discrepancies in the playtime experience. For instance, two youngsters in preschool want to play with the doll wearing the green dress; what do they do to solve the problem? They may both pull on the doll and say, "I want it, give the doll to me." They may even hit each other, and call each other bad names. The teacher should not allow any physical hitting. But, the teacher should be cognizant that negotiations have begun and allow those negotiations to proceed long enough to see if one child says something to the effect of, "I had the doll first." At 4-years-old those words are the beginnings of negotiations in the play experience. The other child may say, "No, I want it now." What happens following these words will clue the teacher in as to whether it is time to intervene. If the process deteriorates, the teacher could then help the negotiation process to proceed in an acceptable manner.

Another component of the socialization process is acquiring friends. Part of this process can be seen to have beginnings in the preschool classroom in terms of peers beginning to learn that interaction and verbal communication require sharing toys as well as sharing experiences. When family members and educators observe youngsters in the process of forming friendships, those adults can gain an understanding of the steps involved in that process. This is part of the broader concept termed *the socialization process.*

Synopsis of Chapter Content

Chapter 1 asks the questions that help us become aware of the total youngster. Who is he/she? What are his/her likes, strengths, disposition, dislikes, desires, and more? Youngsters love to play, and play-yard experiences offer more than just fun for the youngster. Those experiences serve a definite purpose in muscle development, creativity, release of tension, and possibly release of some fears.

What gets youngsters interested in doing something? Some social scientists say that a child's motivation is better served only as an *internal* reward for accomplishing tasks. Others say that *external* rewards and praise do a good service to the person if they are offered in a certain manner. Motivation is discussed in terms of personal attention, internal and external rewards, and the benefits and drawbacks of each method.

How do youngsters learn to make thoughtful choices? What are the benefits of allowing a preschooler to begin to make choices in certain activities? These questions are also examined in this chapter. Will a youngster choose something that is scientific in nature in addition to other activities? Yes, providing scientific activity is also fun and of interest to the youngster. Science is all around the preschool classroom. The innate curiosity in the youngster and the accessibility of natural phenomena help to encourage the child's desire to solve the yet unknown. Why not take advantage of it? This chapter introduces the concept of science. Chapter 8 expands on the science curriculum.

Chapter 2 examines some of the components that help youngsters first recognize, then internalize their responsibility in the process of creating and following policies, which are made up of rules. Youngsters learn that there are consequences when the rules and policies are not followed. It is important that preschoolers help construct the rules at home, and at school, so they begin to understand *why* some of their desires are permitted and others are not. The importance of the youngster's input in arriving at the final policy that the family or preschool classroom has adopted cannot be overstated.

Youngsters want to know from adults how far the boundaries go and the extent to which they can express themselves freely. They want to know the types of behaviors they can exhibit, the ramifications of going beyond the boundaries that were set forth in previous discussions with parents and other authority figures, and what protocol to use in particular situations and why. Children become aware of the consequences of their behavior because adults intervene and remind them.

Chapter 3 involves sharing a meal in preschool, which can be quite different from eating a meal with one's family. The preschool policy of snack and lunch experiences can be different from school to school. This chapter discusses how family practices at mealtime can affect the youngster's understanding of what is entailed in eating a meal away from home through the experience of trying new foods, observing table manners, and assisting in clean-up after the meal.

What is literacy in a preschool program? Chapter 4 examines some of the components of what literacy means at the preschool level, and how literacy is acquired. The discussion, while comprehensive, is not exhaustive. There is an ongoing debate at present as to how the youngster is best exposed to literacy, and then how he/she internalizes literacy. Those experiences that add to the internalization process are also discussed. For example, it is a good idea to have a lot of books in the class library where youngsters can go pick out a book to look at whenever they want to. But that is not enough. This chapter also offers activities that promote literacy behaviors, which include becoming aware that the words on the pages *tell* what is occurring and the pictures *show* what is occurring. Once this awareness blossoms, youngsters usually begin to use pencils and crayons to *write* on a sheet of paper so that they, too, can tell something.

Chapter 5 discusses some of the components of the socialization process that help parents, educators, social scientists, and other adults begin to understand successful peer interactions, both in familial situations and in preschool. Included in the discussion are attachment theory, as this theory relates to the formation of friendships, and language usage, as it relates to friendship. Language has a three-fold function here. One function is discussed as it relates to one-to-one peer interaction, the second function as it relates to the formation of friendships, and the third function as it is included in generating conversation.

Chapter 6 discusses the preschooler in the block area. The multiple levels of cognition that playing with blocks can affect are looked at in this chapter. The stages of handling the blocks and building the structures are discussed from various sources. The scientific and mathematical aspects of playing with blocks are not new to the literature. This chapter adds to the *creative component* of playing with them.

Chapter 7 examines the role of sociodramatic play in the preschool years. The similarities and differences between *play* and *sociodramatic play* are recognized. This chapter also looks at a number of benefits involved in *solitary play* as well as play among peers. There are therapeutic benefits to play that do not necessarily have to be clinical to be effective. In Chapter 7 there is discussion of classroom play that might act as a catharsis for some children. Various other components to play that are vital to the developing young child are discussed as well.

Some of these components of play are: (a) how language is fostered during play, (b) how social skills are developed and enhanced, (c) how negative emotions may be revealed and assuaged, (d) how cognitive development is enhanced, and (e) how themes in play centers may foster longer episodes of play among peers. The examination of the role of play in preschool is currently expanding in the literature, and will continue to be evaluated in the future. This chapter examines and discusses a number of play issues in a comprehensive, but not exhaustive, manner.

Chapter 8 involves the way natural science lends itself to the curious nature of youngsters. It goes into more detail than Chapter 5 does and offers concrete situations and activities. The seasons, insects, and plants are themes or topics that have been found to be conducive to a successful science program in preschool. Science, as it relates to language arts and math, is discussed also. The easy flow of science into projects, graphs, discussions, and more can all be an integral part of the preschool curriculum.

Chapter 9 examines the artistic endeavors of the youngster in preschool. The stages of development in art for the preschooler, according to Smart and Smart (1972), are offered for clarification of the artistic developmental process in young children. Art, as a means of creativity and self-expression, is discussed in terms of possibly reaching a child's emotional needs, especially if the child is shy about expressing those needs.

Chapter 10 discusses math as being pervasive in the environment of the preschool classroom. Basic shapes and colors are seen in fruits, doors, windows, buttons, blocks, and cubbies, just to name a few things. The concept of number, when naturally coupled with one-to-one construction of the concept, can enhance learning in a natural, easy-flowing manner.

The ten chapters in this book offer an in-depth picture of some of the components that can help adults to understand the preschool child. The book can open a way for more study and research in the minds of people interested in furthering the development and understanding of young children.

Chapter 1

Who is the Preschool Youngster?

One aspect of the preschooler's nature is that he/she is innately curious. "Students want and need work that stimulates their curiosity" (Strong, Silver, & Robinson, 1995, p. 10). The preschool child will fully explore new situations involving toys, manipulatives, open spaces, play-yard equipment, and more. This is what leads some social scientists to call young children *constructivist learners*. This means that youngsters manipulate and interact with their surroundings in order to make sense of them. As each child absorbs the environment, he/she is creating meaning for himself/herself. Bologna (1995) stated, "Children use play to construct meaning from and about their environment . . . . Exploration provides young children with a breadth of information about their environment" (pp. 156, 158). A nursery school, preschool, or day-care environment could provide the opportunity for peer interaction.

Importance of Play-Yard Experiences

"As preschoolers grow, they need new outlets for their energy. Threes enjoy releasing their energy by riding tricycles, climbing the steps of a slide, and hopping on both feet like bunny rabbits" (Miller, 1996, p. 20). Success at performing physical activities can give youngsters a sense of power and autonomy. The statement, "I can do that," gives a young child a sense of accomplishment. These activities are engaged in spontaneously; the preschooler does not have to be taught to appreciate the value of exploring. The desire to move, explore, exhibit curiosity, and wonder about the reasons for phenomena is programmed inside the youngster at birth (Bologna, 1995). Lindauer (1993) said we view "the child as an active explorer, discoverer, and manipulator of the environment, as well as a social being" (p. 233). Climbing up and then jumping down is a routine that offers a lesson in gravitational pull and/or the lack of it. For example, when the youngster climbs *up* a rope he/she experiences a heaviness or a force that seems to be pulling down on the body. But when the youngster soars *down* a sliding board, he/she feels almost weightless because gravity is pulling him/her downward (Segal & Adcock, 1986). Youngsters never tire of this experience.

Interaction with the environment is a primary activity for youngsters because of their sense of wonder. They need to know how things operate, so youngsters take things apart to look inside them. A problem may present itself when it is time to replace the pieces correctly. The environment includes the open spaces of the play-yard where gross-motor skills are given an opportunity to thrive. Miller (1997) said, "Through such physical play, preschoolers develop and strengthen their gross-motor skills and experience various aspects of motion, like speed, force, balance, and timing" (p. 38). While participating in the use of large motor skills, youngsters run, climb, reach, pull, and engage in all the other gross-motor movements that keep adults saying with verve, "Don't hurt yourself; be careful!"

Youngsters *must* be active. Wilford (1996) said of youngsters, "They are investigating cause-and-effect and are gaining an understanding of the physical principles involved in motion" (p. 32). Bologna (1995) stated, "[the] teacher plans instructional opportunities that build upon the child's natural inclination to move about, explore, and react to and with the environment. Such a learning environment fosters the development of a proactive disposition to learn" (p. 163). Recess playtime is crucial so that youngsters can expend some of their excess energy. Children seem to be internally driven to challenge their physical abilities. Sometimes they become a little reckless or daring in their exuberance during outdoor play. Adults should be close by to monitor the outdoor recess. Miller (1996) continued about fours:

> Fours use their bodies in more complex ways. They let off steam by performing tricks on tricycles, galloping around the playground, and descending the rungs on the jungle gym. A brisk game of tag allows energy-filled fours to anticipate other players' movements and to experiment with spatial relationships. (p. 20)

Leeb-Lundberg (1974) noted, "In the preschool, the child learns mainly by moving. His movements include running, jumping, stretching, lifting, putting down" (p. 338). Youngsters begin to learn that their bodies can perform many activities that include the display of speed—as in running—and force—as in pushing things around. The play-yard offers the unrestricted space for physical activities to occur. "Play is vital to children's physical development, as it builds such fundamental motor skills as running, hopping, climbing, throwing, and catching" (Brewer & Kieff, 1997, p. 92). At recess in the play-yard, students engage in physical activities that help to keep them fit. Races are run, jungle gyms are climbed—trees too, if they are in the area. When physical play is over and it is time to go back inside the classroom, the youngsters are appreciative of rest-time. This is a natural cooling-down period. Nap time usually follows, and most preschoolers are ready for it.

Play-Yard Experiences and the Development of Cognition

In the play-yard, the cognitive and creative skills can join together to enhance *creative tension*. Creative tension occurs at that moment when the person mentally discovers that something other than what is occurring can happen, or that there can be another way to do a particular project. In this instance, the terms *critical thinking* and *creative thinking* are synonymous. Sometimes another person brings this realization to the fore by challenging what one is doing or saying. Hereford (1997) offered:

> Educators here believe that the presence of a few well-chosen materials can inspire outdoor play that builds and refines cognitive and creative skills. 'We don't view the playground as a totally separate place from the classroom,' says educational director Beth Schneider. 'I encourage our teachers to bring materials outdoors to see what children do with them.' (p. 48)

Water-based paints and brushes taken outside in the play-yard *without* paper initially created a dilemma. The dilemma was purposely planned by the teacher to see if the youngsters would think creatively. When the preschoolers asked for paper, the teacher asked, "Since we're outside, what else can we paint on besides paper?" "Anything," was one reply. The children began to use the water-based paints on the ground, the fence, and the log cabin. They also used the paint on the sliding boards, but the paints did not stick to the metal-and-plastic sliding boards. When asked by the teacher why the paint did not stick, the children told her the sliding boards were too shiny for the paints to stick to them. That was a good preliminary observation by the children. They further said that the sliding boards were too smooth. At that point in the conversation, the teacher explained that the children were exactly right. The surface has to be rough (have friction) for the paints to stick to it.

Plain water with paint brushes can provoke similar experiences, with a *twist*. When the youngsters 'paint' the fence or sidewalks (whatever) with water, the twist occurs when the water dries. Nothing remains! The sun dries the 'water-paint' up and nothing remains. One preschooler exclaimed, "Looka dere, it gone." He was excited because he walked away after liberally splash-painting water on the fence. And when he returned shortly after, nothing but the fence was visible.

Inside the Classroom—Fine Motor Skills

Fine-motor skills are important for manual dexterity. The exercises and activities for development of these skills include grasping small objects; reaching for, holding, pushing, and pulling small objects; and turning the body. These activities can be accomplished inside the classroom, whereas gross-motor skills are better used in play-yard activities. Clay is a very good medium for the development of hand and arm muscles. Children "gain control over hand and arm movements and improve their coordination" (Miller, 1993, p. 34). A secondary benefit is that the creations the children make can be used as a 'Show-and-Tell' project. These creations enable youngsters to begin to grasp the concept of cause-and-effect in terms of actually seeing that when they pound the clay, it gets flat. They discover that if they pinch the clay, it gets little peaks on it. If they roll it around, it becomes either a ball or a snake, depending on their rolling motion. Youngsters see that they can control the shaping of the clay. They can make the clay become something that it wasn't before. The open-ended nature of clay makes it perfect for youngsters who decide to change their creations to something else. "Children have the freedom to change their minds and create anew, because clay can be balled up and used over and over again" (Miller, 1993, p. 32).

After presenting their creations during 'Show-and-Tell,' children, "often like to share their ideas and experiences with you or other children in the group" (Miller, 1993, p. 34). When children share ideas about clay creations they learn that conversation consists of speaking, then listening to the other person speak. This learned pattern of give-and-take—also called speak-and-listen—is fundamental to conversation. Some adults have not learned this fundamental exchange. Some adults *speak a lot*, and *listen a little.*

Legos and bristle blocks are just two of the many fine toys for developing hand muscles and can be used both for table games or floor games. These toys bring eye-hand coordination into the activity of fitting the pieces together, as well as holding the attention of the youngster as he/she creates something tangible. Creations using crayons, pencils, and markers with paper are always popular for self-expression as well as hand-eye coordination.

Puzzles are great in that they serve a number of purposes, both educationally and recreationally. Placing puzzle pieces together aids in hand-eye coordination as well as the *cognitive process of figuring out* why a particular puzzle piece will not fit. Then visually realizing that the puzzle-picture on the table or the floor is the same picture that is on the puzzle box cover is a discovery in itself for youngsters.

Sensory Stimulation

Miller (1997) said it well when writing about how important it is for preschoolers to use and experience the five senses: "They use all their senses to smell, poke, nibble, stare at, or carefully listen to the objects around them" (p. 55). There is special sensory stimulation from the preschool classroom that attracts youngsters and adults alike. For example, a pleasant classroom with color and harmonious arrangement of furniture and equipment is visually attractive. This type of arrangement invites people to enjoyment. It says, "You will have fun here" to the preschooler, who may be initially apprehensive about entering the classroom in the beginning days of school. "Early childhood is an appropriate age for acquiring sensorial awareness, which is critical for the improvement of imagery in memory development and the reproduction of sensations" (Boyer, 1997, p. 95).

Varied textures and manipulatives offer tactile stimulation for children to explore. They can squish their fingers through shaving cream or gelatin, which has been spread over a flat surface. Another medium for finger play is a mixture of flour and water and a drop of food coloring. This mixture makes a gooey-textured loose paste that is great for squishing and making designs on a flat surface. Burlap and felt squares of cloth are great for gluing edges together to make hand puppets, or gluing small pieces of cloth to construction paper to form collages. "Let children enjoy the tactile experience of contrasting textures in a feely box" (Miller, 1997a, p. 54). Making a class quilt is a very popular class activity.

A quiet corner or area for library and story-time circle is ideal for suggesting and promoting a listening attitude and/or quiet dialogue. Children can close their eyes and listen to the sounds of a quiet room. What are those sounds heard even when nobody is speaking? This can be just the beginning of many questions and answers to a listening game. But the game is a cognitive experience in terms of hearing and processing the sound for the purpose of discovering its origin.

Good smells of fruit, pine cones, puddings, flowers, etc., awaken the olfactory sense. Imagine smelling pudding or popcorn when you open the door to the preschool classroom. For children, tasting the good puddings and popcorn is an unmatchable treat while discussing the day's events with a classmate. Gordon and Browne (1989) said, "The young child in the classroom is of the here and now and likes what is familiar and known. The preschooler takes pleasure in common, everyday experiences, learns by doing, and uses all five senses" (p. 74).

Sensory experiences seem to trigger concentration on the individual stimulus that is affecting a particular sense. Thought processes seem to expand to include such questions as: (a) what is that?, (b) can I touch it?, (c) how does it taste?, and (d) is it cold or hot? When the teacher and preschoolers begin to answer these questions and others, cognitive enhancement and extension take place. The interactive socialization process, coupled with the full use of the senses, is paramount in a preschool program. "From birth, children use all their senses along with body movements to explore and keep in touch with their environment" (Bologna, 1995, p. 155).

"Do You Love Me, Ms. Jones?"—
A Look at What Motivates Youngsters

This question was asked by a preschooler who loved his teacher so much that he used to forget that he was in preschool sometimes and call her "Ma." He was so secure and happy in school that he blossomed into the ideal student in social and interactive peer relationships, participated fully in class activities, and was known for his vibrant and jovial friendliness toward his classmates. He was academically and socially ready for kindergarten after his year in preschool. His particular preschool program introduced the youngsters to some letters, numbers, colors, and shapes. They learned songs, poems, and dances also. He had learned to accept challenges and new situations openly and enthusiastically. When his "Ma" came to get him at the end of the day, his parting routine would be to ask, "Do you love me, Ms. Jones?"—Ms. Jones would always answer him by saying, "Right from my heart." What a way to end the school day!

Most children of any age enjoy the emotions involved with experiencing love, joy, and happiness. These three terms are used interchangeably in this chapter. These concepts are psychological by nature, and defined individually according to what each person considers enjoyable. However, there are some general considerations that most children can appreciate. *Positive personal attention* is one such consideration.

Observation of a particular program showed that youngsters enjoyed the personal positive attention given to them by their teacher. Although, a few children did prefer to do things like take hats off their classmates' heads, draw on a neighbor's artwork, or knock down someone's block structure to get *negative attention*. Youngsters displaying inappropriate behavior do present a challenge for the teachers. Daily observations and behavior analysis strategies have to be employed by the teacher to discover how to reach the students who display inappropriate behavior.

Generally speaking, the personal attention given to children by adults does not have to take a lot of time. As an example, in a small group setting, an encouraging or praiseworthy word directed to a particular student about positive behavior can work wonders for that child's self-esteem. For him/her, it is a direct indication that the adult took notice of the effort he/she exhibited to accomplish a positive goal. As adults, we should be cognizant of the *small* effort that can mean so much to a youngster. According to Marshall (1989):

> Provide new challenges and comment on positive attempts. Some children appear to need a lot of encouragement and verbal reinforcement. Encouragement and statements of confidence in the child's ability to succeed may be necessary at first. However, the effects of verbal praise and persuasion may be short-lived (Hitz & Driscoll, 1988). Children will be more likely to benefit by seeing for themselves that they can, in fact, succeed. (p. 50)

Positive attention used as encouragement in preschool doesn't begin to tell the story of what it could mean to a child who is almost constantly being reprimanded for exhibiting inappropriate behavior. It is the adult's hope that the child will come to know that he/she can produce successes, and receive positive attention, instead of displaying contrary behavior and receiving negative attention. Dombro (1995) offered, "Make such comments as, 'You did some good thinking just now about how to reach the ball when it rolled under the chair' " (p. 45). Positive attention "encourages the children to be self-directed problem solvers, and, ultimately, autonomous decision makers" (Zachlod, 1996, p. 50).

Motivation is a concept filled with emotion that begins on the inside of a person, and thrusts that person into a continued, sustained action. Strong et al. (1995) offered "Intrinsic motivation . . . comes from within, and is generally considered more durable and self-enhancing" than extrinsic motivation (p. 8). How, then, does this emotion get started?

One way that motivation can begin is for a mystery or challenge to be presented that the student is interested in solving. "We have stimulated students' curiosity by using a strategy called 'mystery.' We confront the class with a problem . . ." (Strong et al., p. 10). The students need to feel they are capable of meeting the challenge. They need to express their thoughts, try their ideas, and come up with a plan for steps toward a solution. Near successes are *GOOD*. Near successes reveal to students that the possibility for solution is imminent. Strong et al. stated that "students want and need work that enables them to demonstrate and improve their sense of themselves as competent and successful human beings. This is the drive toward mastery" (p. 10).

The manner in which students begin to experience motivation intrinsically may have to do with the orientation of the "goal achievement policy." What goal is one attempting to achieve? Is the goal more knowledge, a higher test score, or both? There is a different perspective on achievement when the goal is to pass a test rather than to learn something that one did not previously know (Collopy & Green, 1995). A student's paying attention in class and concentrating on the homework will result in learning the material. Some students will learn the material to a higher degree than others due to individual ability levels. However, with the emphasis on gaining knowledge, the stress of the test is diminished. But the result will be a grade on the test that is commensurate with the increase in the student's knowledge. The test score increases from learning more, not from worrying about or cramming for the higher test score.

Relating this to preschoolers is not hard to do. When a small group of four members in preschool is provided with flour, salt, oil, green food coloring, and water, the members all know that they are going to learn something that they did not previously know. They do not say to each other, "Gee, we are now going to learn something that we did not previously know." Instead they say, "Ooohhh! What are we going to make?" Implied in that question is—"I don't know something that I will know when the morning is over." No member is thinking, "I have to really pay attention so that I can do this well for a grade, or test score." If the preschoolers were going to be graded, they would all get the scores that reflected their energy and enthusiasm for the project. They would learn the material, which is how to make play-dough, because they were interested in gaining the knowledge. By the way, we definitely do not give *grades* or test scores in preschool.

When the goal achievement policy is centered on gaining more knowledge, the stress level diminishes. There are times when one has to learn information that is not interesting, but is necessary. This does tend to raise the stress level. However, in preschool it is a rare occasion when an activity is not interesting to the eager and willing learners.

External Praise and Internal Motivation

It is crucial that *external* praise by adults, used as encouragement in preschool, is not overdone, nor should encouragement be perceived by the child as insincere. The *internal* motivation and satisfaction that the child receives while accomplishing a goal is what educators and parents hope the child will achieve. The gold star on a chart should not take the place of the internal pleasure preschoolers get when they have accomplished a new task, such as buttoning their coats on their own. "When children are self motivated, they enjoy the activity for itself. Externally motivated behaviors, on the other hand, are usually carried out just to get a reward or some desirable outcome" (Rogers & Sawyers, 1988, p. 7). Adults who provide many opportunities for youngsters to achieve independent tasks and chores are insuring a starting point where preschoolers can begin to experience successes, thereby building self-motivation.

There is much discussion on whether or not it is a good idea to offer external rewards for completion of homework, completion of chores, and other childhood responsibilities because that might send the message that the child should accomplish the responsibilities for external rewards. Some researchers suggest that praise used indiscriminately may do more harm than good. Black (1992) found:

> Researchers agree that ineffective and indiscriminate praise can actually hurt students more than it helps them. . . . Praise had conditioned the children to depend on the teacher for approval, and they were afraid to risk losing it. Brophy, a prolific researcher on this topic, demonstrates that praise is, at best, a weak reinforcer and seldom results in students repeating the praised behavior. (p. 24, 25)

Could it be that *external rewards* can serve the children well in the form of *sincere, specific verbal praise* for their accomplishments? Teachers and parents alike want children to learn to acquire inner motivation, which comes from a sense of accomplishment, rather than depend on them for approval. Researchers Gordon and Browne (1989) offered the following:

> Each time a child is acknowledged, a teacher fosters that sense of uniqueness. 'Carrie, you have a great sense of humor!' 'Freddie, I love the way you sing so clearly.' Saying it aloud reinforces in children the feeling that they are enjoyable to themselves and to others. (p. 406)

This writer has found that praise does have a place in preschool in reassuring youngsters that they have done what is pleasing to themselves and others. The preschoolers' need to please adults can be an extension of their need to please their parents (Mitchell, 1982). This type of reassurance may be specific to preschoolers and early grade students.

Praise, however, can also be viewed as manipulative on the teacher's part. For example, Black (1992) stated:

> P. Bennett looked specifically at what she calls Type A praise—approval statements teachers use to control and manipulate student behavior. . . . 'I like the way Robin is working quietly at her seat.' Not only do such statements single out and compare students, they might be blatant manipulation. (p. 26)

The above controversy and others are currently being debated.

Skinner found, in his experiments with behavior modification, that if behaviors were pleasurable *and* reinforced, the person would exhibit those behaviors over and over again. *Applied behavior analysis and modification* is another term used for behavior modification. The encouraging words (external reward) could be directed toward the *effort* or *behavior* that accomplished the goal, not the goal itself. For instance, "Liza, you have worked hard on the dance routine. That shows the committee you are a serious ballet student." This is a direct praise to a person for effort put forth. To relate this to preschool, "Charlie has put the puzzles on the shelf without being reminded. Now our puzzle shelf is really neat." This statement focuses on Charlie's fulfillment of his duty as the puzzle monitor. The pleasant touch on the shoulder, or the smile from a person whom the child admires, might be just the sign the preschool child needs to encourage his/her efforts at displaying the *appropriate behavior*, at least in the short term. But there seems to be varied opinions and theories in the research literature. This writer recommends continued personal research by teachers, parents, and college students.

The idea of personal attention being sought after by children is not so very different from the adult world. Think of when your supervisor says, just in passing, "Good job done on the Murphy account," when you finally land the big one. Children are susceptible to the same feelings of growth and worth when encouraging words are spoken directly to them.

Just as adults do, youngsters will strive for the praise and recognition from the person in charge. Black (1992) said that three components should be in place if praise is going to work as an encouragement. They are: (a) specificity—which refers to having the praise be specific to an accomplishment, (b) contingency—which refers to praise being contingent on the child meeting the required goal, and (c) credibility—which refers to teachers' facial expression, voice tone, body language, and eye contact all revealing that the praise is genuine. This strategy is not a cure-all, but it can help youngsters build internal motivation.

Making Choices

Ross (1995) explained, "Free choice activities you offer in your early childhood classroom allow children to pose their own questions and pursue their own answers" (p. 42). One explanation of the concept of *personal choice* is a desire to be able to select people who contribute to one's pleasure and/or satisfaction, and to surround oneself with things that are of personal interest and meaning. Being permitted to make choices, even within a limited framework, gives a preschooler a sense of power over the circumstances and events in his/her environment. It further gives him/her a sense of being the important person who is in control of the current situation. Kohn, in an interview conducted by Brandt, said, "You know, kids learn to make good choices not by following directions but by making choices" (Brandt, 1995, p. 16). All of these positive feelings help to create self-esteem in preschoolers, which furthers the concept that their goals are possible. When this concept is encouraged and internalized early in the youngster's life, positive attitudes about almost every endeavor are evident. "I can do it," and "Me, me, pick me!" are exclamations from confident preschoolers. These are the words that teachers want to hear from vibrant students all through the school year and on every grade level. That attitude should begin early in life. Miller (1997b) has found that preschoolers "are beginning to discover what they're good at, what they gain enjoyment from, and what they find challenging and frustrating" (p. 20).

Challenging and frustrating incidents are inevitable. However, the youngster who has a background in which he/she has made personal decisions and choices can pull from a repertoire of strategies to help work through the challenge. This young child can begin to use negotiations that have worked well in previous situations. There has to be a beginning of the 'generalizing process' from one learning experience to another. If a child is allowed to make choices early on, he/she is better prepared to take on new challenges.

"If we want to nurture students who will grow into lifelong learners, into self-directed seekers . . . then we need to give them opportunities to practice making choices and reflecting on the outcomes" (Schneider, 1996, p. 226). Challenge and frustration (within limits) should not be something adults want to protect youngsters from. These two situations offer a *creative tension* that demands answers to unsolved problems. Good! Now the preschooler has to stretch his/her mind to turn the puzzle piece around and over to place it in the spot where he/she thinks it should fit. "Oh no! It doesn't fit there. I'll have to put it this way then, and try it over there." These are good mutterings the teacher wants to hear from the puzzle corner.

When the preschooler experiences the necessity to make a choice, to make a decision about which toy or game to play with, which play group to get involved with at a specific moment, he/she begins to experience self-reliance. The choices and decisions the youngster makes are tied to self-realization and self-determination. This is where the school can reinforce what the parents have introduced in their home environment. Making decisions and choices at home before entering preschool is a good place to start the process. Marshall (1989) suggested, "Give young children simple choices: for example, which task to do first or which of two colors to use" (p. 50).

One can never begin too early to offer the young child choices. It builds self-reliance, which serves to increase courage when the opportunity presents itself to take on even more difficult tasks. To illustrate, after the class has been divided into groups of children who will paint murals for the class play, the teacher now asks someone to paint a special picture of the wolf. The self-confident, courageous youngster will volunteer because of the successes he/she has encountered in decision-making and choice-making. Kristeller (1995) said, "Give children a variety of stimulating choices and then observe how each child discovers his or her own gifts" (p. 35). By the way, the picture of the wolf looked a lot like a truck on stilts. But the child was happy.

In Summary

It is hoped that educators and parents have gained some insight into the preschooler's abilities in physical movement and play, and into cognitive involvement as it relates to physical play. This chapter further attempted to relate the positive influence that words of encouragement and praise can have on the preschooler. Using the five senses in preschool has been discussed here as being one of the important components in a relationship with the environment.

A discussion has been presented concerning the theory that opportunities to make decisions and choices increase self-confidence and self-determination in preschoolers. Making decisions and having choices give youngsters a sense of power and control over particular situations and their immediate environment. In using these ideas and theories with young children, hopefully the adults in their lives will gain more insight so they can better serve the children's needs.

References

Black, S. (1992). In praise of judicious praise. *The Executive Educator, 14*(10), 24–27.

Bologna, T. A. (1995). Integration of the abilities that foster emerging literacy. In C. N. Hedley, P. Antonacci, & M. Rabinowitz (Eds.), *Thinking and literacy* (pp. 153–165). Hillsdale, NJ: Lawrence Erlbaum Publishers.

Brandt, R. (1995). Punished by rewards? *Educational Leadership, 53*(1), 13–16.

Brewer, J. A., & Kieff, J. (1997). Fostering mutual respect for play at home and school. *Childhood Education, 73*(2), 92–96.

Collopy, R. B., & Green, T. (1995). Using motivational theory with at-risk children. *Educational Leadership, 53(1),* 37–40.

Dombro, A. L. (1995). Starting to solve problems. *Early Childhood Today, 9*(5), 45.

Gordon, A. M., & Browne, K. W. (1989). *The roots of prosocial behavior in children.* Albany, NY: Delmar Publishers

Hereford, N. J. (1997). One playground in action. *Educational Leadership, 11*(7), 48–51.

Kristeller, J. (1995). A classroom for every child. *Early Childhood Today, 10*(1), 35–40.

Leeb–Lundberg, K. (1974). The block builder mathematician. In E. S. Hirsh (Ed.), *The block book.* National Association for the Education of Young Children. Washington, DC.

Lindauer, S. L. K. (1993). Montessori education for young children. In J. L. Roopnarine & J. E. Johnson (Eds.), *Approaches to early childhood education* (pp. 243–259). New York: Macmillan Publishers.

Marshall, H. H. (1989). The development of self-concept. *Young Children, 44*(5), 44–51.

Miller, S. A. (1997) Why? when? how come? *Early Childhood Today, 11*(8), 54–55.

————. Why children like what they like. *Early Childhood Today, 12*(3), 19–20.

————. Moving big. *Early Childhood Today, 11*(7), 38, 40.

————. Ants in their pants. *Early Childhood Today, 10*(7), 20–21.

————. Messy play. *Pre-K Today, 7*(5), 32–40.

Mitchell, C. (1982). *A very practical guide to discipline with young children.* New York: Teleshare Publishing Co.

Rogers, C S., & Sawyers, K. S. (1988). *Play in the lives of children.* NAEYC: Washington, DC.

Ross, M. E. (1995). Investigating nature. *Early Childhood Today, 9*(8), 40–47.

Schneider, E. (1996). Giving students a voice in the classroom. *Educational Leadership, 54*(1), 22–26.

Segal, M., & Adcock, D. (1986). *Your child at play: Three to five years.* New York: Newmarket Press.

Strong, R., Silver, H. F., & Robinson, A. (1995). What do students want and what really motivates them? *Educational Leadership, 53*(1), 8–12.

Wilford, S. (1996). Outdoor play. *Early Childhood Today, 10*(7), 31–36.

Zachlod, M. G. (1996). Room to grow. *Educational Leadership, 54*(1), 50–53.

Chapter 2

Some Aspects of the Socialization Process in the Early Formation of Friendships

This chapter discusses the relationship between attachment theory and the development of security as they affect interpersonal relations, in infancy and throughout the child's life. The chapter gives insights into how attachment to parents during infancy, and the security which that attachment fostered, can provide a basis for the sequential accumulation of prosocial behaviors among preschool peers 3-to-5-years-old.

Preschoolers who begin the process of learning to interact with peers one-to-one, then expand their attempts to enter small play groups, are usually successful in forming and maintaining relationships later in life (Hartup, 1983; Katz, 1987; Wilburn, 1997). "Play provides children with opportunities for social development as they learn to share materials with playmates, join play groups, negotiate differences and cope with the disappointment of not always getting exactly what they want" (Brewer & Kieff, 1997, p. 92). Preschool offers youngsters a practical and encouraging environment to play and learn in, an availability of materials, and an opportunity to be involved in situations where they hear their peers' perspective. Segal and Adcock (1986) suggested:

> It is the place where they learn to read social cues and conform to social mores, where they develop their own social style as leaders or as followers. Most important, in preschool, children develop long-lasting relationships with their peers and experience the fun and security of being a part of the group. (p. 200)

Early on, in this progression from one-to-one peer interaction to attempting entry into play groups, the process can be a means of gradually developing the steps required for the formation of friendships in preschool and in the future.

The chapter offers a discussion of the connections among the following constructs: prosocial behaviors, beginning of friendship formation, entry-gaining strategies into play groups, cognitive development as it relates to friendship, use of language as a social function in general, and the further development of language as it relates to friendship specifically.

Attachment Theory as it Relates to Socialization

The young child's willingness, indeed desire, to comply with the parents' wishes and guidelines for acceptable behavior (prosocial behavior), and the child's acceptance of parameters relegated by the preschool for social interaction, are likely due, at least in part, to a successful secure attachment the parent and child have developed during the infancy stages of social development (Smart & Smart, 1972). Meyer offered:

> Attachment is a psychological bond between an infant and her or his primary care giver, usually the mother. Crying and smiling bring infants in contact with care givers and are called attachment behaviors. Attachment provides a secure emotional base from which mature relationships develop. Research shows that inadequate attachment impedes social and emotional development throughout life. For example, when an infant is subjected to maternal deprivation, and thus does not form a secure attachment, subsequent development is often severely atypical. CD-ROM Encarta, Meyer, 1997

The infant develops a secure attachment to the parent when the infant's needs are met regularly and on a consistent basis. When the infant is crying because he/she is wet and hungry, the parent puts a dry diaper on him/her and gives the infant a bottle of milk to drink. In this scenario, the infant's needs are met in a timely and predictable manner. In a nurturing, secure, and fulfilling environment, the young child learns that his/her surroundings are *predictable*, and people can be depended upon for help and guidance (Sroufe, Fox, & Pancake, 1983). The youngster is learning to abstract meaning from the ongoing parent-child relationship and to apply that meaning to situations that are encountered in a social setting, first with other family members, and later with situations involving peers in the preschool setting.

The terms *positive attachment* and *secure attachment* are synonymous. Attachment can provide a basis for discussing the process of developing prosocial behaviors during peer interactions and the formation of early friendships. If youngsters display interpersonal relationships that are negative or nonresponsive, it could be that those youngsters did not have a secure parent-child model to use for abstracting a foundation on which to build peer relationships. But, it could also mean that more time to interact, play, and converse with peers is needed where there is a sizable group of peers with whom to interact.

Generally speaking, youngsters who are securely attached to their caregiver, but who are simply not used to interacting with other children, will more easily learn to work and play well with peers. "Since play is a form of interaction and an integral component of the preschool curriculum, attention must be paid to maximize the positive play behaviors of children" (Wilburn, 1997, p. 1).

There is a difference between an insecure parent-child foundation and a youngster who has simply been raised in a household with adults, and therefore not had the opportunity to learn interpersonal social skills with peers. The child who is just in need of peer companionship will probably adjust more quickly to the interactive process of a shared environment like preschool. Each preschooler takes the time he/she needs to begin to acquire social skills. This is an internalization process that comes with *interactive experiences and time.*

Preschoolers Learn to Share

In a neutral setting away from home, such as a preschool, the youngster can begin the process of adjustment to an environment that is different from the familiar surroundings of home. This adjustment is a learning experience, and the child can use it to exhibit his/her independence and security in interactive relations with teachers and peers (Ainsworth, 1979; Bowlby, 1973). For example, in preschool the young student is likely to begin learning how to share toys with peers and why sharing is important. The preschooler begins to realize that the toys belong to *all* students in the classroom. The teacher and preschool students will have determined, in previous circle-time meetings, the classroom rules for sharing and taking turns using the toys. Essa (1990) stated:

> Before children can share with other people, they must feel secure with their own possessions, knowing that no matter who uses them, the items belong to them. . . . Sharing means that children cannot always have exclusive use of whatever toys they want. . . . Sharing requires a measure of social understanding and development. (p. 84)

At home, when the neighbor's child comes over to play, the youngster without preschool experiences may find it more difficult to share toys and take turns in the play routine because his/her experiences with peers *in a larger play situation is nonexistent.* Mommy may tell the youngster to share; however, sharing is a learned skill as well as an emotional decision. One acquires that interpersonal skill by interacting, not by being told to engage in positive interpersonal skills. The interactive experiences with other children in preschool will prove to be immeasurably more potent than Mommy's words. Experiences help youngsters internalize the *reasons* for positive social interactions. Youngsters are not able to simply intellectualize the reasons for sharing. Leach found:

> Children in neighborhoods where many small children play in and out of each other's yards may have plenty of social mixing readily available. Some children are isolated socially from other children, perhaps because they have no brothers or sisters and live in high-rise apartments or on farms. They may very much benefit, at this stage, from attending a community group, nursery school, or kindergarten. Certainly decisions about preschool education should be primarily based on social practice in being one child among many. CD-ROM Compton's Interactive Encyclopedia, Leach, 1996

Group play is necessary so that the youngster begins to experience the *turn-taking* ritual of *conversation.* Actually *listening* to peers in a group is another skill that is learned as the event takes place. If the turn-taking ritual does not occur on a regular basis, youngsters may continue to have conversations like this: "I want to play wit dis doll [*sic*]!" "My clay thing is a snake." "She my baby [*sic*]." "I can make it looong." "I could put dis dress on my baby." "See, it's real long." "My baby is sleepin' now." This is an excerpt from a recess session in a preschool. Neither child is listening or responding to the other. Both are just expressing *their own* interests.

Group activity does not always run smoothly. If one preschooler exhibits inappropriate behavior in a group, the other peers either accept the inappropriate behavior, or they reject it and require that person to do either of two actions. The person would have to either *leave the group* or *change the behavior.*

Positive peer role models in preschool can be of help in this situation to provide immediate role identification for youngsters who display inappropriate behaviors. Peers usually choose to play with each other when they get along and enjoy the relationship. Successfully interacting with playmates may ultimately lead to the development of lasting friendships for that school year and beyond (Wilburn, 1997). "It may be that preschoolers who develop stable, mutual friendships early in life tend to maintain this type of relationship across ages and show higher levels of social competence during the grade school and adolescent years"

(Gershman & Hayes, 1983, p. 176). It is the desire of parents and teachers to have the youngster internalize and exhibit ongoing prosocial behaviors. This positive attitude fosters and encourages longer lasting friendships.

Development of Friendships

One definition of friendship is what Lawhon (1997) offered: "A mutual involvement between two people that is characterized by affection, satisfaction, enjoyment, openness, respect and a sense of feeling important to the other" (p. 228). Another definition, as the term is used in preschool, is: "A friend is one in proximity, is not hurting you, and is engaged in parallel play. True interactive play is evolving through experience"(Wilburn, 1997, p. 3). Because many youngsters are being cared for outside of their homes in group situations such as preschool, researchers may be better able to gain data from a wider range of youngsters in these different locations.

Piaget and Inhelder found in their studies that infants and toddlers are egocentric. As they grow through various stages, children increase in ability to understand that other people are separate entities from themselves. They begin to learn that those other people may have desires that differ from their own.

Preschoolers are certainly beginning to experiment with the idea of *friendship* (Bjornsen, 1992; Dombro, 1995). Gershman and Hayes (1983) did a study in which they found "the dimensions of general play, common activities, and propinquity comprise major bases of friendship among preschool children" (p. 176). Play and common activities are two mainstays of preschool, providing opportunities for the beginning of friendships. Wilburn (1997) stated:

> The preschool experience provides the means to enrich the child's environment with socialization experiences. Upon entering the preschool environment, socialization will include new people and situations . . . and discussions about life and home experiences, and self-expansion such as socio-dramatic play, sharing, and turn-taking. . . . The socialization process includes gaining entry into play. (p.7)

This atmosphere is conducive to the nurturing of preschool friendships in terms of opportunities for shared activities, conversations, and turn-taking. In a study by Howes (1983) it was found that verbal exchange of ideas and experiences enhanced the formation of friendships in preschool. "Preschool friendships were stable. . . . Preschool friendly interactions were based on verbal exchange . . ." (p. 1050). Initiating an interactive experience by verbally expressing ideas is one means of opening the way for friendships to develop. In realizing that they must actively listen to each other, the preschooler is self-directed into the turn-taking mode of conversation. Friends converse. They are interested in what each other has to say. This is the beginning of that process.

Reciprocity in social interaction is a phenomenon that seems to take place regardless of age. Attili (1990) found that within the Piagetian approach, it has been shown that the reciprocal nature of peer relationships facilitates the understanding of rules regulating social exchanges. Whether preschoolers or older children are together in the play-yard at recess, "the kind of response a child makes to an initiation may well determine whether the initiator will make future overtures" (Quay & Jarrett, 1988, p. 286). A preschooler playing with a floor puzzle responded with "yes" when a peer came over and offered to share her popcorn if the girl would let her help put the puzzle together. It may have been bribery, as well as a friendly overture; but it was a gesture that was received positively. And both girls ate popcorn and solved the floor puzzle together. This is a good outcome of entry negotiation and friendly reciprocity in what Quay and Jarrett termed overture and acceptance of overture in the quote above. Interest in other people, and interaction with other people, usually begins early in life.

During the first two years of life, children are becoming increasingly aware that other people are separate from themselves. Infants' and toddlers' social interaction is comprised of observing the peer's face, smiling at the peer, and reaching for the peer (Bjornsen, 1992; Taleb, 1992). As youngsters begin to recognize familiar playmates, gradually begin to interact, and become aware that actions during play are often reciprocated (Charlesworth & Hartup, 1967), the rudiments of social interactive behaviors are forming. Hartup (1989) noted that "social overtures between nursery school children and their friends commonly elicit continued interaction" (p. 124). This reciprocation is usually the basis for the development of sustained friendships early on.

Children elect to play with peers they enjoy being with, thereby identifying peers who display positive behaviors toward them, and usually avoiding peers who display aggressive and/or other negative behaviors. Thus, a youngster who hits his/her peers with toys in preschool or in a day-care setting is not likely to be popular at play time, limiting his/her chances for making friends. This youngster is in need of peer role models who are usually successful in social interaction. As Kennedy (1992) observed, "Toddlers and preschoolers in day care . . . who were rejected by peers generally had had [sic] less experiences with peers" (p. 40). The continued activity of play is crucial in order to observe those youngsters who need help in developing prosocial behaviors.

When children are *in the process of forming friendships during play experiences,* they can display strategies that allow each other to take turns expressing and reacting to ideas. There is a general verbal give-and-take, an affirmation or rejection of each other's ideas, and a possible redirection or expansion of the interaction as the play session continues. This verbal give-and-take is not always orderly in the usual sense of one person speaking while others are listening. In fact, there may be yelling and pushing occurring during this exchange of ideas. Then, at other times, there may be a semblance of what adults refer to as an orderly dialogue. This writer has been privy to both types of exchanges.

In the process of developing friendships, youngsters will learn to make compromises. In the process of discussing competing ideas, youngsters can begin to *negotiate a compromise.* The negotiations may involve yelling or even fist-fights. The teacher should watch for signs of deterioration, so that fist-fights can be stopped immediately, and a discussion of another way to handle the dispute can follow. But, a lesson in negotiation is in progress. Most youngsters will usually come back to re-negotiate the terms of an agreement and begin to play together once more.

Group Entry as it Relates to Friendship

The opportunity to interact with a peer on a one-to-one basis may help a child who is seeking friendship to overcome a sense of shyness (Segal & Adcock, 1986). Generally, it is easier to form a friendship on a one-to-one basis than to attempt to enter a group setting. Rejection by a potential playmate would seem to be reduced when there is only one other child involved. Therefore, the freer atmosphere in one-to-one relationships seems to encourage even a shy youngster to take a chance and use the opportunity to engage a peer in conversation and/or play. From this step in the process of forming friendships, the youngster moves on to the next step: playing with more than one other person.

Youngsters are learning to make a distinction between *whom they are playing with* and the *process of playing.* For example, if Charles and Henry are building a tower in the block area, and Frank comes over to join them, Frank may not be readily accepted by the two boys. The seemingly rude exclusion of Frank by the first two boys may have its origins in the *ownership* aspect that can be a part of friendship. Charles and/or

Henry may feel an ownership of their current play experience. Miller (1997) noted, "Children become aware that they prefer to play with certain friends during particular activities . . . . Patsy is my friend for dancing but Andrea is my friend for puzzles" (p. 17). For some preschoolers it may be difficult to realize that people do not always need to remain compartmentalized in a friendship. They are learning that many peers engage in one play activity; and one peer can engage in many activities.

Some youngsters need time to go through the rituals of playing, negotiating, creating, and conversing so that they can have interaction with more than one person at a time. Segal and Adcock (1986) offered:

> "Julie's not my friend anymore because she plays with Andrew," Eric complained to his mother. Like other preschool children, Eric could not see beyond the idea of two-person friendship. He could be friends with Julie or friends with Andrew, but if Julie and Andrew became friends, he felt automatically left out. The possibility of three mutual friends eluded him. (p. 185)

It appears that some youngsters feel that when another peer comes into the play experience, *the new child may take the first friend away* (Wilburn, 1997). It takes time and patience for some youngsters to internalize the concept of more than one other person being included in the play activity. This realization eventually comes with extended periods of social peer interaction.

When youngsters begin to have an increasing awareness of ownership of play space, or what Bjornsen (1992) called "protection of interactive space" (p. 19), this can present more play problems. Gaining entry into a group's play space may require the entrant to spend time observing the group's activity to understand what they are doing. Even after having observed the point of reference, it may be that the members are not ready to allow entry. The group members may feel this way because the entrant was not there when the group members *began* to build the block tower, for example. Now that the tower is tall, the original members may feel territorial about it. This is another example of 'ownership of the play experience.' In this situation the entrant will have to verbally communicate and negotiate the terms of entry into the group. Negotiation is an essential social learning growth process.

The negotiation process might be accomplished by including positive comments about the group's activity. This may include offering suggestions about expanding the block tower activity to include a bridge that would connect the first tower to a second tower. In this way, the entrant can make himself/herself an integral part of the expansion process, since the bridge to connect the two block towers was his/her idea. This strategy has strong positive potential for gaining entry (Wilburn, 1997). But it is not a guarantee.

The concept of offering something new, or expanding the activity is potentially valuable to the entrant because it offers a *new vitality* to the play experience for the original group members. *Ongoing* collaboration by the entrant concerning the new idea can be a main ingredient in the process of gaining entry. The entrant's remaining near the group and being unobtrusively persistent in terms of offering information can be a strong factor in helping him/her gain acceptance. However, it is equally true that preschoolers can make nuisances of themselves while attempting to use this strategy. The group members will usually inform an entrant in very specific terms when he/she has overdone the strategy.

Another tactic in attempting entry into the group is for the entrant to use body language and verbal communication similar to that of the group, which is termed *mimicking the group's behavior.* "Imitation serves as a connecting link for some preschoolers" (Miller, 1997, p. 17). In the housekeeping area, if the Daddy is coming home from work, and the family members are joyously welcoming him, the entrant could show enthusiasm by mimicking the group's joyous behavior from the sidelines, without actually intruding directly into the play space. This action may have a positive influence on the group's decision to admit the entrant. *Persistence* and *positive strategies* offer a higher potential for gaining entry than negative name-calling or overwhelmingly aggressive barging-in tactics.

The group members may need time to accept the fact that another person will now be involved in what they are doing. But when the entrant brings a new idea along, which potentially adds to his/her value as a new group member, or when the entrant mimics the group's behavior, the chances are greater for gaining entry. In mimicking the group, the entrant shows interest in the group; but what's more important is that he/she says by mimicking that what the group is doing has merit, that it has importance.

If an entrant has a friend who is already a member of the group, that increases his/her potential for entry even more because the *friend can invite* the entrant into the group, or at the least, speak on the entrant's behalf to the members (Putallaz & Wasserman, 1990). These are all learned strategies that youngsters can internalize by modeling behaviors they have observed in the preschool environment over a period of time. This is not a rapid process. Putallaz and Wasserman made it clear that no strategy is a guarantee of entry. A number of attempts are usually tried before successful entry is gained, if at all.

Friendship and Cognitive Development

Many youngsters involve themselves in solitary play with imaginary characters. This solitary activity can be entertaining and stimulating for the child. However, does it add to increased use of higher-level thinking and social skills? Perhaps. For instance, "The exchange of ideas and resulting disequilibrium involved in peer interaction may serve as a type of brainstorming for the young child" (Dunn & Herwig, 1992, p. 33). Notice the quote says 'peer interaction.' When the youngster is engaged in *solitary play* he/she is indeed interacting with imaginary characters and friends. However, the youngster has complete *cognitive control* over what types of stimulation the imaginary characters and friends are able to produce. There is no outside person to bring challenge or creative tension to the play, and the youngster's complete volition prevails. Cuffaro (1974) observed a young child playing in the block area alone. The girl used wooden figures to represent family members who were engaged in conversation. The girl spoke for all the family members as the scenario evolved:

> Of great importance was that she could regulate the degree of her participation. Without undue pressure, she could select those 'realities' with which she could contend. She could engage in a variety of activities using the variety of identities within herself by directing the behavior of mother, father, baby, and other surrogate figures in her symbolic family. (p. 77)

This play strategy is used often by preschoolers as they engage in self-expression through solitary play. The use of this strategy can also be a catharsis for working through personal problems.

Vygotsky believed that fantasy and imaginary play are governed by rules that are imposed on the play experience by the preschoolers involved, allowing the individual preschooler to abstract meaning from the play situation and generalize the meaning to other play situations. This process of imposing rules that govern imaginary play and fantasy, then the generalizing of those rules to other later situations, is termed *internalization of the rules* by Vygotsky (Bjornsen, 1992). Solitary activity can be an interaction with self for the purpose of extracting sense or meaning from previous interactions with other people. Garton and Pratt (1989) said of Vygotsky's theory:

In solitary activities, children can achieve what they have been learning in inter-action with other people. They talk to themselves as they work towards solution of their tasks. This talk is sometimes termed 'egocentric', in so far as it is . . . not meant for anyone else. (p. 37)

Vygotsky found that the social interaction of children gave rise to the *intrapsychological* discussion (inner speech) at a later time when each child could be alone and ruminate over the previous play experiences (Wertsch, 1990). That would appear to be a potential setting for expansion of critical and/or creative thinking. Wilburn (1997) stated:

Cognitive developmentalists (e.g., Damon, 1977; Eisenberg & Mussen, 1989; Gordon & Browne, 1989) suggest that an internal mental structure interacts with the environment to produce an adapted mental structure. This interaction pro-duces a more sophisticated cognitive structure through assimilation and accom-modation according to Piagetian thought. (p. 7)

This Piagetian thought is in agreement with Vygotsky's theory in terms of the person's internal mental structure being enhanced by additional input, if the additional input resulted in social interaction with people *and* interaction with the environment, as stated in Wilburn's quote. This means that potentially a child could learn to go from *point a* to *point c* when attempting to figure out a situation. He/she would have learned to skip *point b* due to additional information or experiences with other children and with the physical classroom environment. For instance, the young-ster in preschool may begin to realize that he/she doesn't have to always wait for a taller peer to reach up on the shelf to get the puzzle for him/her. After watching the taller child reach up a few times, the smaller child internalizes that *height* is needed. He/she notices that standing on a chair gives extra height. The smaller child has used additional information to restructure his/her thinking strategies. *Point b*, the taller child getting the puzzle for him, has been eliminated because the smaller child now goes directly to stand on the chair for the additional height needed for him/her to reach the puzzle. As Wilburn stated, *the adapted mental structure* has become the *elevated level of mental functioning*, which is the reference to Vygotsky's theory of mental structure being enhanced by additional input of information or knowledge. But it usually includes the social interaction with people as well as environment.

Social speech with peers or adults becomes "internalized while the speech also retains its communicative functions. Social speech becomes totally integrated into the development of the child's practical intellect, ultimately leading to the development of cognitive processes" (Garton & Pratt, 1989, p. 38). Vygotsky noted that as social interaction occurs between two or more peers, *higher psychological functions occur* as part of each child's *intrapsychological* inner speech, as the child rethinks the situation. This rethinking process helps to form cognitive/behavioral repertoires within the child to be used in future experiences. Garton and Pratt said of Vygotsky's theory:

> Intellectual functioning takes place on the social plane to start with, then proceeds to the individual level. The child internalizes the mental processes initially made evident in social activities, and moves from the social to the individual plane, from interpsychological functioning to intrapsychological functioning. (p. 36)

In concurrence, Goodman and Goodman (1990) said research indicated "that peers of similar knowledge or ability cause reorganization of concepts as students argue and negotiate their solutions to various problems" (p. 228). This reorganization of concepts is taking place in what Vygotsky referred to as the interpersonal, social plane. To this writer, the implication is that peers interacting to gain meaning from *classroom* lessons, and young children interacting to gain meaning from *play-group* situations, *both* have the potential to argue and negotiate their solutions to their various problems. To negotiate is to participate verbally. Church (1992) observed:

> Asking someone to think about something invites him to take ownership in the process and encourages higher-level thinking. Piaget once said, "Teaching is not telling." In other words, children, especially young ones, can absorb only a small amount of information when it is told to them. But when they participate in such activities as problem solving and thinking creatively, they learn much more. They are taking an active role in constructing their own knowledge. (p. 62)

The negotiation process gives rise to reorganization of concepts, and the possibility for intrapsychological inner speech to occur, which has potential for the formation of an inner directory of cognitive/behavioral interactive skills from which preschoolers can choose the appropriate behavior to fit a situation.

According to Wilburn (1997), "the use of objects as representations of the pretend characterization in play can be interpreted as use of symbolic encoding strategies used to enhance cognitive development" (p. 8). As an example, this writer was privy to a play situation in which one peer was pretending to be HeMan, the good guy, while another peer was pretending to be Dragon, the bad guy. HeMan and Dragon were engaged in a pretend war. Harry wanted to have Dragon win a war sometimes, while Bob never wanted Dragon to win a war because he said that bad guys are not supposed to win. The two peers had to negotiate the terms of the play experience, thus producing creative tension of the psychological higher functions that Vygotsky spoke of. The boys used negotiating skills to come to an agreement, and after much arguing, the play experience continued.

Having to critically think through their problem, both preschoolers' *cognitive processes* fostered the *reorganization of concepts* about the two characters. They also rethought their ideas about good characters always winning and bad characters always losing. The moral issue is a valid concern, but it is beyond the scope of this chapter. The fact that the youngsters were critically thinking and reorganizing their concepts during the play session is the point.

Another example this writer observed occurred in the housekeeping area. A preschooler of smaller physical stature than her peers wanted to be the mother during a particular session of play. The other child, who was usually the mother, told the smaller peer, "You be the baby because you little [sic]." The smaller girl responded, "Everybody's Mama ain't always big, because my Mama ain't big. She's little."

The tension was in place, and the girls negotiated back and forth. The result was an argument that the teacher intruded upon, with the best of intentions. After listening to both children's explanation of the situation, the smaller girl was allowed to be the mother by the teacher. However, the intrusion by the teacher may have been premature, because perhaps the girls could have reorganized the structure of their own cognition, given the new information the smaller girl had offered about mothers not always being big. The girls may have solved their problem themselves through continued conversing and reasoning. If they could not have eventually solved the problem, then the teacher should have intervened. Unfortunately, the teacher did not give them enough time for the process to reach its conclusion. She was not comfortable with the children engaging in debate. Perhaps she saw it as too confrontational. Sometimes the debates and negotiations get loud in preschool. Debates still should be allowed to occur, under the watchful eye of the adult. Gibson (1989) offered:

> Social conflicts, I realized once again, provide needed opportunity for children to practice skills in negotiating and taking responsibility for themselves. For teachers, they provide moments in which to describe and define the nature of our social system. As a result, these episodes should be welcomed rather than avoided. (p. 43)

In concurrence, Jacobs (1997) observed preschoolers interacting in the play-yard. He realized that disagreements are bound to occur in the natural course of social interaction. He offered these observations:

> Conflicts will inevitably arise from time to time. When they occur, don't rush in to solve the problem for children. If they never confront problems, they'll never learn to solve them. Indeed, it's when children are in conflict with others that they have the best chance to develop the vital skills of perspective-taking, self-regulation, and negotiation. (p. 53)

Negotiation will not always be a smooth running process. But it is a necessary process for youngsters to engage in. It is imperative to remember that preschoolers are just beginning to learn the skills of negotiation. Some youngsters have been present during family discussions and/or disagreements. Other youngsters have seen family members argue, fight, and hurt each other. Therefore, the teacher must be near and observant in case the children's negotiations deteriorate into abusiveness.

Use of Language in the Formation of Friendships

The discussion process that takes place between youngsters as they interact is an integral part of language and comprehension development. As the preschooler becomes more effective in the use of symbols (talk, gestures, and other forms of body language, rules, props, etc.) to communicate meaning *to* others around him/her, and as he/she becomes more adept at interpreting, understanding, and internalizing meaning *from* others toward himself/herself, the preschooler is said to be in the process of becoming more cognitively and socially aware (Bjornsen, 1992; Lubeck, 1985).

"Once children can communicate meaning in social interactions, relationships take on a quality of continuity, as children respond to the impact that meanings and symbols have in the context of different relationships" (Bjornsen, 1992, p. 14). This seems to mean that relationships between youngsters can grow in depth and can potentially continue to develop into full friendship, once the youngsters experience the clarity and richness of communicative language using expressive, expository symbols and body language.

Consider this scenario: Two youngsters are playing together in the housekeeping area. Susan says, "I like playing with you today, Tina, because you are not hitting me." Tina replies, "I'm not hitting you because you let me be the Mommy again." Susan and Tina are getting along fine at this point because Susan is compliant with Tina's wishes. But it appears from the dialogue that once Susan stops being compliant she will be hit again by Tina.

Contrast that scene with this one: The setting is the same. Susan says, "Sometimes I want to be the Mommy when we play in the housekeeping area, but today I'll be the Titi (it means aunt and is pronounced teetee). Next time it'll be my turn to be the Mommy because today you're the Mommy." Susan is expressing how she feels about the play arrangements that have gone on previously between herself and Tina, with Tina always being the Mommy. The *language usage* in the second scene implies that Susan had to *think deeply* about the previous play experiences and treatment she had been receiving from Tina. Susan felt the need to communicate her thoughts to Tina. Tina replies, "I like to be the Mommy because I like to rock the baby and tell her stories." Susan responds, "You can rock the baby next time when you are the Titi because Mommies don't always have to rock the baby. Titis can rock the baby too."

These two youngsters have successfully negotiated terms for future play. Whether or not the future play works out as they have just planned is irrelevant for the purposes of this discussion. The point here is that *the girls have used thoughtful, expository dialogue with give-and-take strategy.* The negotiations have potential for being the solution to Susan and Tina being in an abusive situation whenever they play in the housekeeping area (Berg, 1990; Wilburn, 1997).

One benefit of sociodramatic play is that language communication can be fostered and encouraged in preschool experiences so that it begins to promote logical thinking skills as youngsters attempt to sequence events and evaluate situations using cause-and-effect reasoning (Cliatt & Shaw, 1988; Isbell & Raines, 1991). It appears that Susan and Tina may have a solution to their particular problem because Tina really just likes to rock the baby-doll and tell her stories. That seems to be the reason she previously insisted on being the Mommy. Susan recognized that fact and told Tina that Titis can also rock babies. The cause of the problem (Tina's wanting to rock the baby) led to the effect (her abusive situation with Susan). The preschoolers appear to have negotiated terms that can potentially alleviate the negative and abusive aspect of their relationship.

Preschoolers are beginning to learn to *recognize the meaning* that the other person is attempting to convey so that the interaction or conversation can proceed smoothly. For instance, in building the block tower, Edward tells Joel, "You can play with me." Joel is happy to hear this and proceeds to enter the block area. Joel attempts to put a block on Edward's tower, but Edward protests, "Stop that, stop it." Joel exhibits confusion, then says, "But you said I can play with you." Edward responds loudly, "Yeah, but I meant you could build your own stuff with the blocks; don't put blocks on *my* thing." Edward was inviting Joel to engage in *parallel play*, not *interactive play*. Edward did not make his *meaning* clear to Joel until Joel attempted to play.

What has taken place between Edward and Joel is a component of group dynamics in which someone speaks, and the listener (or listeners) has misinterpreted the meaning of what was said. This happens in the natural course of events in the daily lives of adults and children. One cannot guarantee freedom from this phenomenon because human error does take place. However, there are skills that may aid in lessening the potential for misinterpretation of what has been said. To illustrate, the *speaker* can be specific and detailed when conveying his/her thoughts into words. The *listener* can remain focused and attentive to this encoding of the speaker's thoughts. Hopefully, with both parties doing their parts to convey and receive meaning, the correct or intended meaning is internalized. This writer is pleasantly surprised that the intended meanings get transferred from *speaker-youngster* to *listener-youngster* as often as they do. Otherwise, there would be more tears and fist-fights in the play-yard than are currently occurring. These are sophisticated skills that preschoolers are in the process of learning in the natural environments of the home and preschool.

Conflict in Friendships

"The ability of preschoolers to interact with peers in the classroom setting in such a manner as to foster friendships and create an atmosphere conducive to positive group interaction is a critical developmental task" (Wilburn, 1997, p. 11). This quote is the ideal situation that preschool educators strive to achieve. However, conflict is a natural part of the socialization process, and socialization is a part of friendship development. During conflict, a youngster who is trying to wrest a toy from a peer can learn that his/her peer feels just as strongly about the toy as he/she does. Rybczynski and Troy (1995) stated, "disputes among children may be inevitable. . . . Let the children settle as many of these differences as possible on their own, which will teach them conflict resolution skills. The teacher need only intervene if necessary" (p. 11). The youngster may resort to inappropriate behaviors (spitting, name-calling) as coping strategies or face-saving strategies due to frustration brought on by not getting the toy from the peer. It may be that the youngster has seen this behavior in his/her out-of-school environment and is mimicking it, or it could be that the youngster is still in the process of learning that others may not always allow his/her desires to prevail. He/she is in the process of learning how to *control his/her behavior.*

Preschoolers generally begin to interact because they are in agreement with each other. They have come together to play. Conflict can occur when one person begins to disagree with the action or conversation. Laursen and Hartup (1989) did a study in the natural setting of the preschool classroom where the conflict was resolved without teacher intervention. In that study, one preschooler was insistent upon a certain outcome and the other child acquiesced. "One of the strongest predictors of behavior after the conflict was whether or not the children were interacting affiliatively before it began. Children who were interacting before the conflict tended to continue interacting after the conflict . . ." (p. 293). One child gave in to the ideas of his/her peer.

That study seems to indicate that when youngsters who are already friends have a conflict, one friend will take the conciliatory position and give in to the wishes of the other peer so that play can continue. "Youngster dyads demonstrated high levels of conciliatory resolution behaviors during those conflicts . . . that did not involve aggression" (Laursen & Hartup, 1989, p. 294). Youngsters tended to resume the play activity more frequently if they had *developed a friendship* before the conflict and were not *just acquaintances* (Laursen & Hartup, 1989).

Overly aggressive behavior may have its origins in the outside life of the preschooler. In an effort to understand extreme aggressiveness, which is defined as hurting or attempting to hurt others verbally or physically, an explanation of two aspects of aggression may shed some light. Siegel (1990) identified what he termed background anger (anger displayed at home in the presence of the youngster), as well as certain videos exhibiting extreme aggressive patterns seen by the youngster, as contributing factors in a child's aggressive, conflictive behaviors. Background anger could include parental arguments in the presence of the child. "These two conduits of anger may be a cause of emotional internalization of aggressiveness, which can express itself through impulsive actions by some students" (Wilburn, p. 28).

The family is the primary teacher of the youngster, with the greatest influence on his/her early childhood behavior (before peer pressure encroaches). The family environment can give clues and insights into the youngster's behavior. With educators gaining an understanding of how that background knowledge can affect the child, help can be offered by educators so that the youngster can begin to learn to manage his/her aggressiveness.

In Summary

It appears from one train of thought called 'attachment theory' that children who have developed a secure attachment to their primary care-giver have a much better chance at achieving and maintaining friendships. Educators can be watchful for students whose prosocial behaviors can be used as role models for those students who are displaying inappropriate behaviors in play situations.

In an ideal situation, preschoolers are being taught language communication skills at home by their family members; in preschool by interacting and conversing with their peers, teachers, classroom aides; and in other social settings where interaction is taking place (Lubeck, 1985). Youngsters learn language through interaction with adults and peer models who engage them in conversations, and with adults who read to them and supply them with vocabulary and verbal sentence structure as the need arises. Youngsters ask questions, experiment with vocabulary usage, and learn to become proficient in language communication during all these processes (Antonacci, 1994).

This is in keeping with Vygotsky's *zone of proximal development* in which the more knowledgeable role model is helping preschoolers to build upon what they already know, and what they have been in the process of learning from infancy to the preschool years. Young children are receiving instruction and imitating models at home and in school, thus gaining knowledge of vocabulary, language structure, and other oral cultural phenomena. The cognitive developmental process begins after immersion into the social, interactive, and role-modeling experiences have begun to occur because the entire socialization and cognitive processes are continuously occurring and intertwining (Vygotskian in theory; Hedley, 1994).

References

Ainsworth, M. D. S. (1979). Infant-mother attachment. *The American Psychological Association, 34*(10), 932–937.

Antonacci, P. (1994). Oral language development. In P. Antonacci & C. N. Hedley (Eds.), *Natural approaches to reading and writing.* Norwood, NJ: Ablex.

Attili, G. (1990). Successful and disconfirmed children in the peer group: Indices of social competence within an evolutionary perspective. *Human Development, 33,* 238–249.

Berg, D. N. (1990). The role of play in literacy development. In P. Antonacci & C. N. Hedley (Eds.), *Natural approaches to reading and writing* (pp. 33–48). Norwood, NJ: Ablex.

Bjornsen, C. A. (1992). *Friendship and social competence in preschool children.* Unpublished doctoral dissertation, Virginia Commonwealth University, Richmond.

Bowlby, J. (1973). *Attachment and loss: Vol. 2 Separation.* New York: Basic Books.

Brewer, J. A., & Kieff, J. (1997). Fostering mutual respect for play at home and school. *Childhood Education, 73*(2), 92–96.

Charlesworth, R., & Hartup, W. W. (1967). Positive social reinforcement in the nursery school peer group. *Child Development, 38,* 993–1002.

Church, E. B. (1992). *Creative thinking-flexible fun! Pre-K Today, 7*(2), 62–63.

Cliatt, M. J., & Shaw, J. M. (1988). The story-time exchange: Ways to enhance it. *Childhood Education, 64,* 293–298.

Cuffaro, H. K. (1974). Dramatic play-the experience of block building. In E. S. Hirsh (Ed.), *The block book* (pp. 69–88). National Association for the Education of Young Children. Washington, DC.

Dombro, A. L. (1995). First friendships. *Early Childhood Today, 9*(4), 44–45, 47.

Dunn, L., & Herwig, J. E. (1992). Play behaviors and convergent and divergent thinking skills of young children attending full-day preschool. *Child Study Journal, 22*(1), 23–32.

Essa, E. (1990). *A practical guide to solving preschool behavior problems.* Albany, NY: Delmar Publishers.

Garton, A., & Pratt, C. (1989). *Learning to be literate.* Oxford, UK: Blackwell Publishers.

Gershman, E. S., & Hayes, D. S. (1983). Differential stability of reciprocal friendships and unilateral relationships among preschool children. *Merrill-Palmer Quarterly, 29*(2), 169–177.

Gibson, L. (1989). *Literacy learning in the early years through children's eyes.* New York: Teachers College Press.

Goodman, Y. M., & Goodman, K. S. (1990). Vygotsky in a whole-language perspective. In L. C. Moll (Ed.), *Vygotsky and education* (pp. 223–250). New York: Cambridge University Press.

Hartup, W. W. (1983). Peer relations. In E. M. Hetherington (Ed.), & P. H. Mussen (Series Ed.), *Handbook of child psychology, Vol. 4 Socialization, personality, and social development* (4th ed., pp. 103–196). New York: Wiley.

———. (1989). Social relationships and their developmental significance. *American Psychologist, 44*(2), 120–126.

Hedley, C. N. (1994). Theories of natural language. In P. Antonacci & C. N. Hedley (Eds.), *Natural approaches to reading and writing* (pp. 3–18). Norwood, NJ: Ablex.

Howes, C. (1983). Patterns of friendship. *Child Development, 54,* 1041–1053.

Isbell, R. T., & Raines, S. C. (1991). Young children's oral language production in three types of play centers. *Journal of Research in Childhood Education, 5*(2), 140–146.

Jacobs, P. J. (1997). How to head off conflicts. *Early Childhood Today, 11*(7), 52–54.

Katz, L. G. (1987). Early education; What should young children be doing? In S. L. Daman & E. F. Zigler (Eds.), *Early schooling and the national debate* (pp. 151–167). New Haven, CT: Yale University Press.

Kennedy, J. H. (1992). Relationships of maternal beliefs and childrearing strategies to social competence in preschool children. *Child Study Journal, 22*(1), 39–60.

Laursen, B., & Hartup, W. W. (1989). The dynamics of preschool children's conflicts. *Merrill-Palmer Quarterly, 35*(3), 281–296.

Lawhon, T. (1990). Encouraging friendships among children. *Childhood Education, 73*(4), 228–231.

Leach, P. (1996). *Child development.* [CM-ROM]. Excerpted from Compton's Interactive Encyclopedia. SoftKey Multimedia, Inc.

Lubeck, S. (1985). *Sandbox society.* London, UK: The Falmer Press.

Meyer, J. W. (1997). *Infancy.* [CD-ROM]. Microsoft Encarta 98 Encyclopedia. Microsoft Corporation.

Miller, S. A. (1997). Bathroom talk. *Early Childhood Today, 9*(5), 46.

Minuchin, P. P., & Shapiro, E. K. (1983). The school as a context for social development. In E. M. Hetherington (Ed.), & P. H. Mussen (Series Ed.), *Handbook of child psychology, Vol. 4 Socialization, personality, and social development* (4th ed. pp. 197–274). New York: Wiley.

Putallaz, M., & Wasserman, A. (1990). Children's entry behavior. In S. R. Asher & J. D. Coie (Eds.), *Peer rejection in childhood* (pp. 60–89). New York: Cambridge University Press.

Quay, L. C., & Jarrett, O. S. (1988). Social interaction styles of socially normal, low-interacting, and socially–emotionally handicapped preschool children. *Child Study Journal, 18*(4), 285–294.

Rybczynski, M., & Troy, A. (1995). Literacy-enriched play centers: Trying them out in the real world. *Childhood Education, 72*(1), 7–12.

Segal, M., & Adcock, D. (1986). *Your child at play: Three to five years.* New York: Newmarket Press.

Siegel, W. F. (1990). *Fostering prosocial behavior in preschool children through teacher, student, and parent involvement* (Report no. PS-018-753). Nova University. (ERIC Document Reproduction Service no. ED 318 568).

Smart, M. S., & Smart, R. C. (1979). *Children: Development and relationships.* New York: Macmillan.

Sroufe, I. A., Fox, N. E., & Pancake, V. R. (1983). Attachment and dependency in development perspective. *Child Development, 54,* 1615–1627.

Taleb, T. F. A. (1992). *The relations between children's self-concept and prosocial behaviors.* Unpublished doctoral dissertation, University of Maryland, College Park.

Wertsch, J. V. (1990). The voice of rationality in a sociocultural approach to mind. In L. C. Moll (Ed.)., *Vygotsky and education* (pp. 111–126). New York: Cambridge University Press.

Wilburn, R. E. (1997). *Prosocial entry behaviors used by preschoolers to enter play groups in the natural setting of the classroom.* Published doctoral dissertation, Fordham University, New York.

Chapter 3

Parameters and the Preschooler

This chapter discusses the relationship between the youngster's growing ability to understand and adhere to family policies, parameters, and rules that govern social behavior *in the home,* and *outside of the home.* The terms *preschooler, youngster,* and *young child* all represent children between the ages of 3-to-5-years-old.

The chapter further discusses some reasons why the parent or other adult allows the young child to become involved in setting parameters for what is expected and allowed. Parameters are also called *boundaries* and *limits* in this chapter. It is important that the child and adult discuss the *responsibilities* attached to any special requests made by the child that are out of the ordinary. Included in this discussion should be a reminder of the *consequences* that follow when rules are not adhered to. One example, if the preschooler knows that he/she should play with toys in his/her room, but asks to bring the toys into the living room, his/her responsibility will be to take the toys back into his/her room when play time is over. If the toys are not taken back into the room, it will be suitable for the child to have consequences that follow the infraction.

The design of the chapter is such that questions are posed, followed by a discussion of practical situations. Theory is introduced to support the discussions, which begin to shed light on possible answers to the questions.

Parameters and Social Interaction

Why is it important for parents to set parameters and rules to govern young children's behavior? One reason is that preschoolers are beginning to recognize and understand the ramifications of their behaviors when they interact with other people. The concept of discipline is similar to the concept of guidance in that the adult is trying to lead/guide the child into positive experiences and reaction patterns. The word discipline is a derivative of *disciple,* defined as a person who follows a leader (Mitchell, 1982). The way parents respond to situations involving the child's discipline has an effect on the child's growing awareness of his/her role in the community of the family.

This awareness carries over into the school experience. Zachold (1996) said, "I have learned that children thrive when given appropriate responsibilities in the classroom; it gives them a sense of ownership and self-confidence" (p. 51).

Living in a family can be similar to living in the wider community in a sense, because what one member of the family does can have adverse effects on all other family members, if parameters and rules are not followed. For instance, if a child leaves toys in the living room, other family members must then step over them to use that room. The child should be aware from previous family discussions that toys are to be taken back to his/her room or put in a specific area after the youngster uses them. If he/she leaves the toys where they do not belong, a verbal reminder can be given to the youngster concerning clean-up time. The child should then be held responsible for immediately putting the toys away with no negotiations. Gordon and Browne (1989) offered:

> In preschool and kindergarten, a teacher allows children to take initiative and does not interfere with the results of those actions. At the same time, teachers and parents provide clear limits so that the children can learn what behaviors are unacceptable to society. (p. 104)

Gordon and Browne implied above that the youngster's actions will have results. Those results will be evaluated in terms of the clear limits the teacher and/or parent have discussed with the youngster previously. The youngster learns by experience, which of his/her actions are acceptable. This is an experiential approach. But the crucial component in this approach is that the youngster and the authority figure have previously discussed the responsibilities and rules, along with the consequences for infringement on those rules. To illustrate, after establishing with the youngsters that all of the blocks in the block area belong to everyone in the class, the teacher may pose questions as a strategy to illustrate the rule. One question might be this: "When Charlene is building in the block area, can Fred go in and build with some of the other blocks?" "Can Fred take Charlene's blocks away from her to put them on his building?" Some teachers have found that during these discussions the youngsters give appropriate responses, but have a different sense of a situation when they are actually involved in a real-life situation. The child who answers,

"Charlene should let Fred use the other blocks to build," may not want a peer to enter the block area when he/she is in there. That is why the *experiential approach* to learning is fundamental to helping young children internalize as they learn.

Preschoolers may come up with a large number of rules when given a chance to express themselves. They tend to be very specific in terms of situations. Preschoolers have not mastered the skill of generalizing one situation and then applying that generalization to a similar one. The teacher can act as guide at this point and help the youngster consolidate the rules down to a workable number. Stone (1993) stated:

> A young child will more easily remember just two or three key rules. Explain them in simple terms that your preschooler or kindergartner understands. Reviewing the rules from time to time—not just when a rule is broken—will help your child learn what kind of behavior is expected. (p. 10)

When a serious parental attitude about parameters and rules is in place, the youngster has much less trouble beginning to realize *reasons for rules* as they affect interactive relationships. Consistency in discussing the explanations for the parameters and rules is crucial because when children have a verbal exchange, they tend to internalize meanings, thereby coming to peace with the rules potentially more quickly than children who are merely told what to do. Youngsters can begin to generalize and apply the perspectives their parents have expressed to them when they enter the preschool environment. An example, when Mommy says, "Pick up the toys from the living room and take them to the toy shelf" at home, then the child may have less trouble when the teacher says, "It is clean-up time. Let's put the toys away now." In that sense, the youngster is beginning to learn that rules apply at home and at school. It is, therefore, crucial for the youngster to be aware of the rules and understand the consequences of not adhering to them. *Consequence* is not a threatening term. It is a part of the natural sequence of events in life.

Rules and Cognitive Adaptation

How do youngsters begin the cognitive process of selecting which action they should take when there are conflicting or divergent paths they could use to accomplish their goals? One answer is offered by Piaget, and later Kohlberg, who agreed that the progression from one "moral stage to the next is the result of the interaction of the maturation of the organism and experience. The maturation of cognitive capacities is critical because judging and evaluating right and wrong are primarily active cognitive processes" (Eisenberg & Mussen, 1989, p. 122). This quote appears to mean that the young child learns to internalize moral stages as a result of overlapping between social experiences and the natural maturation process. The natural maturation process involves growing both physically and mentally. These two processes working together seem to foster the cognitive developmental process so that the youngster gradually becomes able to judge and evaluate what is right and what is not right.

The process and progression are usually developed in terms of what the child has been previously exposed to, according to Eisenberg and Mussen. What the youngster internalizes when he/she is involved in social situations can be mentally stored. The mentally stored internalized situations act as models that the youngster can retrieve for use in later situations (Vygotskian in theory).

Nourot (1993) offered, "Moral development too, has its roots in the play of young children as they develop empathy and come to understand the rules and roles of society" (p. 19). An interesting example of the *lack* of judgment and lack of the development of empathy in an interactive situation in a preschool setting is as follows: A young boy entered preschool on the first day of school with the rest of the students. The morning began with introductions and table games.

In the days that followed, the class routines and rules were developed by the preschoolers, with the teacher's guiding help. Those rules and routines were then discussed in circle-time and repeated daily so that they became almost like a rhythmic chant to the beat of "One, Two, buckle my shoe." Internalization of the rules for interactive behavior is a gradual process that allows youngsters to *gain meaning as they encounter situations where the rules and routines apply.* Everything is concrete and contextual learning at the preschool level.

The preschoolers were settling into the daily activities of school. However, the boy showed problems from the first day in terms of displaying quiet, aggressive behavior. He began hitting his peers, although he was not overly loud, and he did not run around the classroom in an overly excitable manner. He seemed to be calm and observant. To be frank, he displayed really bizarre behavior.

On this particular day, the boy entered the block area during playtime and began to build a structure. He would hit the other preschoolers whenever they attempted to get some blocks that he wasn't using, to build something for themselves. He was reminded by the teacher of the rules to share the blocks. Rather than share the blocks with his classmates, the boy soon left the block area and sat alone at the table. All the while he was nonverbal. He did not respond to the teacher when she attempted to converse with him.

All of a sudden, he got out of his chair without any obvious provocation and went over to an unsuspecting girl who was engaged in conversation with her friends, and hit her on the arm. The girl shrank away from him out of surprise and fear. McNeilly-Choque et al. said, "Tommy enjoys hitting and teasing Paul for the fun of it. Paul does not have a toy or anything that Tommy wants. Tommy just likes using Paul as his personal punching bag" (McNeilly-Choque, Hart, Robinson, Nelson, & Olsen, 1996, p. 50). This quote seems to exemplify the attitude of the boy in preschool. He seemed to enjoy the girl's reaction because his face exhibited a happy expression, almost a smile.

It was his habit daily, even prior to this particular incident, to hit peers who would not hit him back. Whenever the boy hit someone who did hit him back, he would not hit that person again. The discipline technique used in this particular preschool was the *time-out chair*. The boy would be taken to the chair and reminded why he had to sit there. He was told to think about the class rules concerning helping and sharing, and about the rule that stated "never hurt each other." Essa (1990) said, "Calmly take the child who hit to the time-out area. Firmly but quietly say, 'I cannot allow you to hurt other children. You have to sit here until I tell you that you may get up' " (p. 32).

When the teacher or aides asked him why he would hit the other children, the boy would answer that he liked to hit them because he could make them cry. It appeared that their crying was a source of pleasure for him because his facial expression revealed what could be taken as a pleasurable expression. His parents were told daily, beginning on the first day of preschool, about his behavior. Whitaker said:

> The child may consistently hurt others. . . . You have kept the parents informed all along, but by now have become convinced that your joint efforts haven't been successful and their child needs outside help to overcome her difficulties and be happy and successful in school. . . . Discuss the child's strengths and state clearly what the problems continue to be. Review what you have all done in the past including previous meetings. (1995, p. 12)

The parents seemed to be at a loss as to what to do. This writer does not know if the parents were the boy's natural or adoptive or foster parents. They were asked if there were incidents outside of school that might precipitate this type of aggressive behavior. The parents denied knowing about any reasons for this type of behavior by their son. Kennedy (1992) suggested, "Parenting variables may have either an indirect or direct effect on peer social relations. The indirect model suggests that early family experiences result in an orientation to the social world that generalizes over time" (p. 40). The boy's parents seemed genuinely concerned. They said they were actively discussing his school behavior with him.

Other parents began to inquire and complain about the boy's treatment of their children. The boy was counseled by the preschool teacher and aides (there was no psychologist involved at preschool), but to no avail. As Gordon and Browne (1989) stated, "One of the most negative social behaviors is aggression. It is this type that Albert Bandura researched, finding that much of it is learned by watching others" (p. 107). Could it have been something the boy observed in his out-of-school environment? Maybe. The boy's parents said they spoke to him about his preschool behavior every evening when they got home, and every morning before bringing him to preschool.

The boy was paired with more outgoing, active youngsters in group activities. He would not usually hit them because they would hit him back, hard. The boy would stand near the group members and observed their activities for a time. He would then walk away from that group to hit an unsuspecting peer who would not hit him back, but who would either cry or tell the teacher.

The boy's parents were eventually asked to remove him from the preschool. They were advised to discuss his behaviors with his pediatrician for recommendations and evaluation, which was beyond the scope of that preschool setting. He was in preschool about 3 months before being asked to leave. This writer thinks 3 months was too long to have the other children subjected to the bizarre behavior of the boy. Mitchell (1982) offered the following statement concerning a child who was biting other children in a preschool setting:

> When a four or five year old bites it is even more important to look for the cause. This is the manifestation of a deeper problem. Something is going on in this child's life which is disturbing him enough to set his world ajar, and like thumb sucking and masturbation, his behavior is a means for expressing his anxiety. (p. 52)

One could consider the circumstances of the boy in the narrative similar to the child who bites in the quote by Mitchell. It would appear that both of these behaviors need close observation, supervision, and perhaps even professional evaluation.

Needless to say, the boy did not display any understanding of sharing toys or treating peers with empathy (Bjornsen, 1992; Nourot, 1993). He showed no internalization of the rudiments of learning to share, learning to implement the class rules, or learning to make judgments as to what was right and not right in the preschool setting. The boy also showed no interest in the staff's efforts to guide him to observe and emulate his peers in preschool as they were learning to share and cooperate with each other. He would be invited into a group, only to hit someone or move out of that group if the members were of a mind to hit him back. What was the boy feeling about himself? Dudek (1994) suggested:

> Many children lack the ability to express themselves in appropriate ways because the adults in their world do not have the time or the skills to teach them. Nor do the adults realize that teaching self-control is important to help improve the way children perceive themselves. (p. 4)

Very possibly there were extenuating circumstances in the boy's life outside of preschool that prompted his behavior. This example serves to show that there may be some children who *will need more help than the classroom environment and teacher can provide*. Since the parents said they were also conferencing with the youngster at home to no avail, they should then talk to the pediatrician about a plan to get help for the child.

Parents' roles are so important in fostering the idea of what is acceptable interactive social behavior. Parents assume role model responsibility as they deal with family situations in a consistent and fair manner, and as they set parameters for their children's activities. In this way, youngsters come to recognize a framework on which to base their own judgments of what is appropriate and what is inappropriate. Mitchell (1982) offered:

> He *wants* to please the adult who holds the key to his security, he *needs* to feel the approval of that person, but how can he know what will win it for him when the rules change every day? . . . What is the key to this all-important consistency? How does a parent go about achieving it? Set the ground rules, in your own mind, decide what standards of behavior are important, and how you can enforce them." (Mitchell, 1982. p. 36)

For instance, if it was against the rule yesterday to take cookies from the jar without asking Mommy, then it is still not a good idea to take cookies without asking Mommy, even though she isn't looking. The child is learning to differentiate between what is right (obeying Mommy) and what is wrong (not obeying Mommy) because Mommy is never happy when the child takes cookies from the jar without asking her first. This lesson is basic, and with repetition, can usually be internalized by the youngster without much trouble.

Mitchell (1982) gave this example: "How often do we as parents and teachers teach our children to do the very things we punish them for? We yell or shout at them in angry tones and then we scold them for engaging in shouting matches with their peers" (p. 3). In our effort to teach a youngster appropriate behavior, adults have an obligation to *exhibit* the behavior that they are talking about. The old adage, "Do as I say, not as I do," still doesn't work.

At the preschool level, conformity to rules is being internalized by the youngster according to what pleases or displeases the parent or other authority figure. The preschooler is not usually concerned with the *reasons* or intentions of the person who did not follow the rules, just that the person did not follow the rules. To illustrate, take the following situation. Snack-time was just about to begin. One of the class rules, established by youngsters and teacher, was that nobody could begin to eat his/her snack until everyone was served. This was a table manners rule. Liza and Joe are youngsters at this preschool. On one particular day Liza drank her juice as soon as she sat down, before everyone had been served. Joe yelled at her for not following the rules. Liza said she had the hiccups and needed to drink to make them go away. Joe insisted that she wait until everyone had snack before she could drink, hiccups notwithstanding. At this point the teacher began to explain that Liza could have gotten a drink of water from the fountain to help get rid of her hiccups. She further explained to Joe that Liza had an emergency that required a drink immediately. Joe conceded to Liza drinking the water but not the juice.

The class was being introduced to real-life situations that happen often, and that have to be addressed in ways that may not follow the rules explicitly. Kristeller (1994) said. "Often, very literal fours who thrive on order create rituals and rules that have to be followed exactly" (p. 61). The word *fours* in the above quote refers to 4-year-old youngsters.

Preschoolers can be quite pedantic when learning about rules. The youngsters' understanding of circumstances surrounding reasons has not developed at this stage. The ability to actually discern *why* one action or decision is good and another action is not, will take time to develop as preschoolers experience situations where they can make choices. As youngsters mature chronologically using interactive and communicative skills, and as they are helped through the decision-making process when unsure of what to do and why, their understanding of *reasons for actions* will mature.

Group Reinforcement of Parameters

What could be a reason why a youngster is rejected by his/her peers? When a preschooler is rejected by peers, one reason could be that he/she is behaving in an inappropriate manner. The rejection is a type of parameter reinforcement that the peer group itself can execute. When group monitoring does not help the rejected youngster understand that his/her current actions are the problem, an adult can help. However, the adult should not intrude too quickly, but allow the negotiating process to begin. Preschoolers need time and interactive experiences to learn techniques for figuring out how to negotiate their difficulties in socially acceptable ways (Wilburn, 1997).

Members of the group may begin to yell at the peer who is behaving unacceptably. From the yelling stage, that peer may realize that he/she has caused the problem, and begin to repair the inappropriate behavior. The adult would not want to short-circuit that most vital step in the interactive process. However, the adult does want to be cognizant of a situation that might be deteriorating into uncontrollable behaviors such as fistfights or loud screaming.

One way preschoolers learn the social skill of negotiating difficulties is to imitate role models around them (Bjornsen, 1992; Taleb, 1992). For example, when adults disagree about something they usually have a discussion. This exchange of ideas may result in a compromise of the original plan, with elements of both the original ideas and new ideas. Or, an entirely new plan may evolve.

Preschoolers can learn that verbal communication can lead to the solution to problems, in an environment where adult role models interact through discussion. Young children can choose from a number of responses when they have had a background of verbal interaction with adults, with family members, and with peers. Thus, negotiation skills, through active verbal communication, may begin to take priority over hitting each other to settle differences. It is a good beginning to a life-long process. Some *adults* still hit each other rather than verbally negotiate. We want to help youngsters learn early in their lives that hitting is inappropriate.

Discipline and the Preschooler

What does it mean to discipline a young child? It does not only involve guiding the social behavior of the youngster. Discipline has other components, such as (a) developing an understanding of the feelings (emotions) of others, (b) beginning to understand the ramifications of deliberately hurting others, and (c) beginning to learn the consequences he/she will face for deliberately disobeying the rules previously established for given situations. It may take a while for youngsters to learn to generalize the rules to other situations. The adult will have to have patience and encourage the youngster in this process.

It may be difficult for some adults to think that any preschooler could willfully and decidedly go against the established rules, but it can occur with some children. "We need to be more demanding of our children, but in a gentle and loving way. We need to say more often, 'Sorry, but you'll have to accept the consequences'" (Rasch, 1997, p. 576). When children decide to be contrary, there are consequences to those decisions.

Discipline also encompasses the steadiness and consistency that should be evident in the adult's *interaction with* the child and *supervision over* the child. Discipline implies parameters (limits). Mitchell (1982) noted that the word *discipline* stems from the word *disciple,* which implies that adults want youngsters to follow (discipleship) policy (rules). When adults discipline children, they must be cognizant that they provide a good example for the youngsters to follow. "Limits are a necessary part of any group or society. . . . They are protective structures that help children feel secure . . . help people know how far they can go" (Gordon & Browne, 1989, p. 196).

Discussion of the *whys* for the various parameters is necessary between child and parent, even when the reasons seem obvious. The purpose for the discussion is to make sure the child has an opportunity to express himself/herself as the parameters are being worked out. Logical consequences for not following the rules, or for not observing the parameters, should be a part of the discussion. However, for preschoolers to begin to learn what consequences mean when they do not follow the classroom policy, it may be necessary to model the cause-and-effect relationship. This could be accomplished by having preschoolers role-play situations involving class rules. They sometimes monitor each other in this manner by pointing out in which role-play situations the rules were followed and in which situations the rules were not followed.

Since circumstances may change, it is imperative that the preschooler be reminded of those rules often. Youngsters are learning so many new things that they tend to forget to follow rules, and they forget the consequences of not following them. This forgetting is different from willful defiance. Mitchell (1982), speaking of young children, stated:

> It makes them uneasy when an adult abdicates from their [sic] authority. They
> need to be able to press against the security of boundaries, and know that they

will remain firm. "I know my mother (teacher) will not let me" feels better than a
shaky, "who will stop me if I go too far?" (p. 38)

Often there will be a meeting of the minds between adult and child. Sometimes there will be disagreements. But, at the least, the youngster and the
adult will have discussed what the parameters, rules, responsibilities, and
consequences are concerning the routines in preschool, home, and else-
where (Gordon & Browne, 1989). However, it is important that the adult
make every effort for youngsters to have enough time to discuss the rules
and parameters, that many modeling situations be observed by the youngsters so that visual representation will have occurred, and that active role-
play situations about what is expected of them in the preschool context
are also observed. "By the time they were through offering their ideas, most
of the children had the rules very well in mind" (Mitchell, 1982, p. 141).

Extenuating circumstances that may warrant a change in the parameters can be discussed as the case arises. These extenuating circumstances
should *not* be allowed, by the adult, to occur often because the child may
see it as a way to manipulate the rules. The manipulation technique may
or may not occur on a conscious level in the child's mind.

It may be helpful for the child to have responsibilities associated with
granting his/her requests. For instance, "You can spend the night at Aunt
Jane's house if you complete your homework before we go over for sup-
per tomorrow evening." This implies *completion* of the homework at
home is the deciding factor for the overnight visit.

At the preschool level, part of setting parameters should include offering an alternative mode to the play situation. As an example, if flipping
sand onto the floor is a problem, the teacher can place funnels, plastic
bowls, and various sizes and shapes of containers in the sand-bin for the
youngsters to use for pouring and measuring the sand. These mathematical activities may take the place of throwing or flipping the sand. Another
built-in parameter to throwing and flipping sand is to dampen it before
the youngsters begin to play with it. This helps because the sand sticks
together.

Another example of the need to set parameters occurs when youngsters do not want to leave an area or stop an activity when it is time to
move on to something else. The youngster might say, "But I don't want to
eat snack now because I'm still riding the bike."

Preschoolers may get so involved with their present activity that a
sudden change can cause them to get angry or become confused and
frustrated. One way of preparing the child for the upcoming change is to
announce that the change will occur in 5 minutes, so that the interruption

in the play experience is not sudden. The child may still protest, but the forewarning may alleviate a full tantrum. If the full tantrum does occur, the other classmates can go on to the next activity, leaving the tantrum-child exhibiting the tantrum-behavior. When he/she grows tired of that behavior as he/she sits alone while everyone else is involved in the new activity, that youngster should still be held to the established routine of the preschool classroom. This means that the tantrum-child has to proceed to what the rest of the class had to do before moving on to the present activity. If the teacher surrenders the routine to the tantrum-child's whims, the teacher has to be ready to surrender other routines to other youngsters. At that rate parameters and rules, as a whole, will eventually be relinquished.

Routines and Rules Can Be Grounding Agents

Are routines boring to young children? No. Routines can be valuable to youngsters as a grounding agent. Since the concept of time is abstract, routines can give the day's events and activities a point of reference. Most youngsters can internalize the preschool daily routine in this way: first, we have snack, then we play, then we hear a story, then Mommy comes for me after the story. The daily repetition (routine) is predictable and comforting, bringing to the youngster a sense of control over situations in his/her immediate environment. "You got to have routines so they know what's next," said Ms. Holmes (Kilborn, 1997. p.1) in an article in *The New York Times*. Ms. Holmes is a home-care provider with six children in her charge.

Rules, as well as routines, can offer a grounding effect during peer interaction. As play evolves, youngsters can create the rules that govern the situation. For example, "I'll be the Daddy and I'll cook the dinner." "No, because the Daddy don't cook; the Mama do [sic]." This is part of a dialogue from a recess playtime in a preschool classroom. The rule was established between the two preschoolers that Mamas cook and Daddies do not cook for that episode of play. "If the rules are mutually agreed upon, the rules may be internalized . . . rather than externally imposed" (Rogers & Sawyers, 1988. p. 50). Church (1997) stated:

> Acknowledge children when they apply rules equally to all. Kindergartners' interest in rules is a sure sign of maturity. With your patient guidance and support, learning to make and follow rules will serve them well next year in the grades. (p. 40)

Emotionally, the sense of predictable routine can bring with it a strength that allows the young child, who used to cling to the parent, to eventually say, "OK Mom, you can go because I know you will come back for me after nap time." When the preschooler has arrived at this level of realization, he/she has begun to internalize the security that predictable relationships and environments, with established routines, can help to create. That is a big step in the process of becoming comfortable in environments where Mommy is not present. In September, when parents see their child crying because Mommy and Daddy are leaving, it is hard for the parents to realize that a separation adjustment is in progress. The child will usually adjust and accept the reality that Mommy will come back to get him/her, after he/she has experienced that routine.

In Summary

Parameters, routines, discipline, responsibility, and consequences are all realities of social living that the preschooler has to learn in order to live in society. This chapter offered some aspects of helping the youngster cope with the transition from egocentricity, when everything appeared to revolve around his/her whims and desires, to learning about other people's desires, to learning interactive skills. It appears that *reasons* for parameters, rules, responsibilities, and consequences *discussed at home* helps to make the transition to preschool easier and with fewer problems.

References

Bjornsen, C. C. (1992). *Friendship and social competence in preschool children.* Unpublished doctoral dissertation, Virginia Commonwealth University, Richmond.

Church, E. B. (1997). Moving big. *Early Childhood Today, 11*(7), 39–40.

Dudek, A. (1994). *Teaching self-control.* NCEA Notes/November. Department of Elementary Schools. San Antonio, CA.

Eisenberg, N., & Mussen, P. H. (1989). *The roots of prosocial behavior in children.* New York: Cambridge University Press.

Essa, E. (1990). *A practical guide to solving preschool behavior problems.* Albany, NY: Delmar Publishers.

Gordon, A. M., & Browne, K. L. (1989). *Beginnings & beyond.* Albany, NY: Delmar Publishers.

Kennedy, J. H. (1992). Relationships of maternal beliefs and childrearing strategies to social competence in preschool children. *Child Study Journal, 22*(1), 39–40.

Kilborn, R. T. (1997, June 21). *Child-care solutions in a new world of welfare.* The New York Times, pp.1,20.

Kristeller, J. (1994). It's my game. *Early Childhood Today, 8*(7), 61.

Lubeck, S. (1985). *Sandbox society.* London, UK: The Falmer Press.

McNeilly-Choque, M. K., Hart, C. H., Robinson, C. C., Nelson, L. J., & Olsen, S. F. (1996). Overt and relational aggression on the playground: Correspondence among different informants. *Journal of Research in Childhood Education, 11*(1), 47–67.

Mitchell, G. (1982). *A very practical guide to discipline with young children.* New York: Teleshare Publishing Co.

Mize, J., & Cox, R. A. (1990). Toward the development of successful social skills training for preschool children. In S. R. Asher & J. D. Doie (Eds.), *Peer rejection in childhood* (pp. 338–361). New York: Cambridge University Press.

Murphy, J., & Miller, S. A. (1997). How children make friends. *Early Childhood Today, 12*(1), 16–18.

Nourot, P. M. (1993). Historical perspectives of early childhood education. In J. L. Roopnarine & J. E. Jonson (Eds.), *Approaches to early childhood education* (pp. 1–32). New York: Macmillan Publishers.

Rasch, B. W. (1997). Consequences—A forgotten concept. *Phi Delta Kappan, 78*, 575–576.

Rogers, C. S., & Sawyers, J. K. (1988). *Play in the lives of children.* National Association for the Advancement of Young Children. Washington, DC.

Segal, M., & Adcock, D. (1986). *Your child at play: Three to five years.* New York: Newmarket Press.

Stone, E. (1993). How to prevent power struggles. *Scholastic Parent and Child, Nov/Dec,* 10–11.

Taleb, T. F. A. (1992). *The relations between children's self-concept and prosocial behaviors.* Unpublished doctoral dissertation, University of Maryland, College Park.

Whitaker, R. (1995). When a child needs outside help. *Early Childhood Today, 9*(5), 12–14.

Wilburn, R. E. (1997). *Prosocial entry behaviors used by preschoolers to enter play groups in the natural setting of the classroom.* Published doctoral dissertation, Fordham University, New York.

Zachlod, M. G. (1996). Room to grow. *Educational Leadership, 54*(1), 50–53.

Chapter 4

Sharing Meal Time Experiences in Preschool

As preschoolers enter social situations that are different from their experiences at home, they will begin to encounter a healthy, progressive, and worldly change in many familiar rituals and celebrations. That is, they will begin to realize that everyone and everything does *not* occur in the same manner as it occurs in their home environment. One of the rituals that may be different from home is engaging in eating a meal in preschool. Branen, Fletcher, & Myers (1997) stated, "Many children eat one or two meals and two snacks a day outside the home and away from their parents" (p. 94). Eating is a shared interpersonal encounter that opens new opportunities for the youngster to experience the way people outside of his/her home handle the event of having a meal together. This realization can fill the youngster with apprehension because the situation is not yet familiar to him/her.

New Eating Experiences in Preschool

Frequently, when meals are eaten at home, the youngster eats what the parent gives him/her. The child may pick and choose from among the food items on the plate, but the youngster eats what the parent provides. Parents usually prompt their children to try the variety of food items on their plate by saying how nutritious the food is, or maybe that dessert is contingent upon the child at least tasting the food at mealtime. However, in some homes, the child eats what the parent substitutes when the youngster has refused to eat the original food. Yes, there are some households where the youngster gets to say what he/she will not eat, and then Mom fixes what the child wants to eat. Segal and Adcock (1985) asked this question: "Are fewer arguments about food at dinner because the children get to choose, more or less, what is served to them?" (p. 48).

In many preschools, the youngster is given the healthy choices of the preschools' nutritionists. The preschooler then has the choice of eating some parts of the meal, all of the meal, or none of it. That is where student choice enters the situation. Branen, Fletcher, & Myers (1997) said:

> Meals were served to the children at scheduled times, and the children were free to choose what and how much they would eat from the provided foods at each meal. . . . Researchers concluded that successful feeding of children is best accomplished when adults provide a variety of healthful foods. (p. 90)

In some preschools the variety of substitute meals is limited. The substitute is given when a doctor's note states that the youngster is allergic to the scheduled lunch of the day. For special dietary rules, the parents of some preschoolers may be asked to send their child's lunch and snack to preschool. These are special cases of health and/or religious regulations.

Consider this scenario: "My child is a picky eater," says Mrs. Jones to the director of a preschool, while the parent and director are interviewing each other prior to the child being enrolled in the preschool. "We will introduce your child to new foods, as well as to new social experiences, here at our preschool," replies the director. The parent still has misgivings and says, "I prefer to send lunch for Heather because I am worried that she will not like the lunch here. She is used to having what she likes to eat, and because she is a picky eater, she may not eat well here." Segal and Adcock (1985) found in a study they conducted that "the rule might be that Heather is not required to eat any particular food at dinner time" at home (p. 48). The quote seems to imply that the child is given what she wants to eat when the family eats dinner. Perhaps the family meal is planned around the child's learned behavior, which is to express what he/she wants for dinner. Or it could be that the family eats a planned meal, and Mom fixes something different for the youngster. A child from a household similar to this one may have difficulties in preschool at mealtime.

Eating away from home is a real concern that some parents express to directors and teachers frequently. The procedure that follows should be discussed by parents and directors prior to enrollment so that parents realize and understand the preschool's policy concerning lunch and snack.

Parents should provide the preschool with a list of foods the child is allergic to so that the child's health is always a consideration. Sometimes, a doctor's note is required to attest to the child's allergies. A menu for the week or month could be provided to parents so that a substitute can be given to the child when a food that he/she is allergic to is going to be served. The substitute lunch can be sent in by the parent or the preschool may provide it. Eating the preschool lunches could be seen as a growing, maturing experience for the child that is a part of learning about the broader scope of life outside of the home environment.

Some preschools are more liberal than others, and do allow parents to send lunch and snack for picky eaters. But other preschools consider it a part of the early education social curriculum to introduce new foods to the students, and do not allow parents to send food from home. This should all be discussed before the youngster's enrollment in the preschool.

Gentle Coaching by Peers and Teacher

One way the director can help assuage this type of parental concern is to offer advice based on long-standing previous experiences with the eating behaviors of youngsters who have been enrolled in that particular pre-school. As an example, the director could inform the parent that *most* youngsters coming into this preschool, some of whom are picky eaters, tend to watch the other youngsters at the table and see that their peers are tasting and enjoying the new food. Youngsters observe that the other children are eating the lunch and conversing about the activities of the day in preschool, and are generally having a positive, social meal experi-ence. This may influence the picky eater.

Heather, the picky eater, now has visible evidence that other young-sters are enjoying the lunch. This might be enough to convince her to taste some portion of the lunch, and eventually to eat all, most, or at least some of it. Many youngsters want to conform to the flow of their peers' behaviors so as not to seem contrary or odd (Smart & Smart, 1972). This type of conformity usually occurs with the majority of students, rather than contrary behavior.

But there may be some students who still do not eat. Heather may need more time to decide about eating the preschool lunch. Poole (1997) offered, "For some preschoolers, food offers an opportunity to assert their power and control" (p. 20). Heather may need time to realize that she does not have the control (power) in preschool that she has at home over the meal time experience. The first realization by youngsters that life is not necessarily the same in preschool as it is at home may have the effect of a *rude awakening on the child*. The experience can be seen as a process encouraging emotional growth in the youngster. With teachers, aides, and parents working together to reinforce the *positive* aspect of Heather eating the preschool prepared meal, the youngster may learn to eat her lunch with fewer problems as time passes. What are some of the ways teachers, aides, and parents can help reinforce the positive aspect of eating the prepared meals in school?

Let us say that Heather does not attempt to try the lunch, even though the others are eating. The teacher can now approach the table and remark about how happy he/she is to see that "this table is enjoying the lunch." This table is the one where Heather is sitting, not eating her lunch. But the other students are eating at least some portion of their meal. The teacher may say, "Heather, you might want to try some of the food on your plate so that you can tell Mommy how delicious your lunch was today in preschool." This is called *gentle coaching*.

It has been known to work in many cases. Borgia (1991) observed the same method used by teachers working with preschoolers in Italy and noted, "It appears that they use gentle coaching techniques when they work with the children" (p. 20). The teacher can walk away after speaking the gentle coaching words. This may be the gentle urging that makes the difference because now the child is "given an opportunity to make a limited choice" in what she is going to eat (Segal & Adcock, 1985, p. 51). The limited choice is that the teacher said that Heather *might want to try some* of the food on her plate. The other preschoolers may now take up the mode as coaches and begin to tell Heather how good the spaghetti and meatballs taste, and that she should try them. Her peers are being models for Heather in this social interpersonal environment (Bjornsen, 1992). Heather may try the spaghetti and meatballs at this juncture because mild peer pressure is now at work (Eisenberg & Mussen, 1989).

If Heather still has not attempted to eat anything on the lunch plate, the last attempt at gentle coaching from the teacher might be to remind Heather that afternoon snack is "waaaay" after story-time circle. The reminder should stress that she will probably be very hungry by then if *she chooses* not to taste anything on her plate. In this way the youngster now feels that she has ownership or power to make the eating decision (Dombro & Wallach, 1988; Gordon & Browne, 1989).

Heather may not really understand that she will get hungry between lunch-time and snack-time. She probably does not realize that there will be *no* food given to her in that interim. Once she has had that experience, that might be the concrete component that helps to solidify in her mind that there is no food between lunch and snack-time.

The teacher can now begin to name the items of food on Heather's plate: good bread, yummy spaghetti and meatballs that Mommy said Heather eats at home, tasty string beans, and pears for dessert. Notice that there has been no *confrontational* component to the gentle coaching used in preschool. The confrontational approach could have negative ramifications for Heather in terms of her possible rebellion, *and* for the rest of the preschoolers, in producing a harsh atmosphere during the otherwise pleasant meal-time experience.

But then again, this type of gentle coaching may provoke the following kind of reasoning in Heather's mind: "I'm not going to get a replacement of this lunch. Most of my classmates have completed the meal. The teacher is not going to ask me what I want to eat, like Mommy does sometimes when I don't want what she gives me. I might get real hungry by story-time circle. Maybe I should try the spaghetti and meatballs." Of course, Heather will not think in these sophisticated terms to herself, but she may think the essence of these words. This is the outcome hoped for by the preschool teacher.

However, there are times when preschoolers like Heather do not touch the lunch. In that case, the teacher goes forward with the regular clean-up routine, with the preschoolers bringing their empty plates to the garbage bag. Heather will, of course, throw her uneaten food in the garbage bag. And she will get her snack after story-time circle. Chances are that Heather will be quite happy to receive her snack. Mitchell (1982) said:

> A normal, healthy child will not starve if he misses a meal. In fact, when the attention ceases to focus on him he will probably eat what you put before him. He may not eat as much as you think he should, and he may not choose to eat it in the order you suggest, but he will eat when he is hungry. (p. 39)

In concurrence, Essa (1990) stated, "If the child has eaten little during the meal and then tells you he is hungry a while later, do not lecture about his not having eaten. Also, do not provide any food. Simply tell him when the next meal will be" (p. 393).

Natural consequences of one's actions occur daily. The natural consequence of a youngster putting a hairpin into a socket is that the child could be electrocuted. Therefore, neither parent nor teacher would allow that natural consequence to occur. However, one can see the logic in the way Evans (1996) summed up the inevitable result of a student not eating his lunch:

> The principle of *natural consequences* is that reality can influence a student's behavior more than the teacher can. For example, a young boy who decides not to eat experiences hunger. He soon learns that eating lunch is to his own benefit. (p. 83)

Perhaps it will take only one such meal-time experience as described above to convince Heather, and preschoolers like her, to engage in eating at least some portion of the lunch in preschool. That is the desired outcome that teachers and parents hope to accomplish.

In Summary

All the new situations that youngsters encounter outside of the home may not be *easily* assimilated into their previous circumstances (Bullock, 1988). However, they are now beginning to experience how people other than their family members perform certain tasks and rituals. In this chapter, a youngster is experiencing the meal time ritual at preschool. The new experiences will help to enrich and expand the youngster's view of life and help to prepare him/her for acceptance of new events, interactions, and occurrences outside of the familiarity of the home environment.

References

Bjornsen, C. A. (1992). *Friendship and social competence in preschool children.* Unpublished doctoral dissertation, Virginia Commonwealth University, Richmond.

Borgia, E. (1991). *Impressions of reggio emilia.* ED 338 386. Microfiche.

Branen, L., Fletcher, J., & Myers, L. (1997). Effects of pre-portioned and family-style food service on preschool children's food intake and waste at snacktime. *Journal of Research in Childhood Education, 12*(1), 88–95.

Bullock, J. (1988). Understanding and altering aggression. *Day Care and Early Education, 15*(3), 24–27.

Dombro, A. L., & Wallach, L. (1988). *The ordinary is extraordinary.* New York: Simon and Schuster.

Eisenberg, N., & Mussen, P. H. (1989). *The root of prosocial behavior in children.* New York: Cambridge University Press.

Essa, E. (1990). *A practical guide to solving preschool behavior problems.* Albany, NY: Delmar Publishers.

Evans, T. D. (1996). Encouragement: The key to reforming classrooms. *Educational Leadership, 54*(1), 81–85.

Gordon, A. M., & Browne, K. W. (1989). *The roots of prosocial behavior in children.* Albany, NY: Delmar Publishers.

Mitchell, G. (1982). *A very practical guide to discipline with young children.* New York: Teleshare Publishing Co.

Poole, C., Miller, S. A., & Church, E. B. (1997). Why children like what they like. *Early Childhood Today, 12*(3), 19–22.

Segal, M., & Adcock, D. (1985). *Your child at play: Two to three.* New York: Newmarket Press.

Smart, M. S., & Smart, R. C. (1972). *Children: Development and relationships.* New York: Macmillan.

Chapter 5

Budding Literacy Acquisition
and the Preschooler

The family unit is primary in teaching the youngster what he/she learns before entering preschool. "The family provides the basic experiences that have a profound effect on children's early cognitive development" (Sigel, 1993, p. 181). Fox (1997) stated:

> The child who comes home from playing with a neighbor and says, "That boy, he don't play fair!" needs to hear a parent say, 'Oh, so that boy doesn't play fair?' Young children still see their parents as their most reliable models. By the time they reject their parents and willingly turn to peers, their language patterns will have been set. (p. 240)

All of the cultural and social components of living in a family have an effect on the literacy the child absorbs either serendipitously or by direct instruction from family members or close friends. For instance, seeing older siblings reading books and doing homework has an impact on the youngster as an important and serious event. As the child sees family members reading newspapers, singing from hymnals in church, reading the Bible or other religious material, and reading novels for pleasure, the child begins to realize that reading books and talking about what is inside those books is a positive activity. "Homes in which books are present familiarize children with the purpose of books and ways to use them, thus providing school-relevant skills very directly" (Snow, 1983, p. 185). York (1995) expressed it this way:

> Literacy, the process of learning to read and write, begins at home. It does not officially begin at a particular age; it develops as children gain experience with language and print and learn the purposes for reading and writing. (p. 30)

The strategy of *questions and answers* is familiar to youngsters before they enter preschool. Youngsters are always asking questions as they search for knowledge and understanding of their surroundings. At home, parents and children engage in this type of conversation often. In fact, the question and answer strategy can be seen as the basic type of conversation between parents and youngsters. However, when the child enters preschool the strategy begins to shift. The shift is away from the child being able to direct *all* questions to the adult, and the child receiving *immediate individual* answers. *Some* direct questions are answered by the adult immediately, while other questions may be answered in a more general way due to the number of children in preschool. Even when the teacher is engaging in direct conversation with a preschooler, the amount of time is not as long as when the parent and child converse with each other at home.

The apparent change for the youngster is that he/she now has to wait and listen as the teacher talks to other children and attends to their questions, answers, and conversations as well. Waiting one's turn is a learned behavior. Preschoolers usually receive all the attention at home. Having to wait for attention is a learning experience that is also a growth experience. The outside world offers different experiences from those that preschoolers engage in at home.

Children and family members engage in questioning and answering each other for the purpose of exchanging information on an extended, in-depth basis. This fosters the exchange of information that goes beyond the immediate content. This is a form of oral history. Take this hypothetical instance. A mother and child making cookies can move on from discussing cookies to the information about the grandmother who taught the mother how to make cookies. *But grandmother owned a sweet-shop where she sold the cookies she made long ago. With the money from the sweet-shop grandmother invested in a small company.* That is how there was money to reinvest and become financially comfortable. All of this knowledge came from an extended conversation with questions and answers.

Emerging Literacy—From Home to Preschool

Children who are read to at home on a regular basis come to preschool wanting to engage in the story-time circle routine of listening as the teacher tells the class what the story is about. The teacher reads, then stops and discusses the story with the preschoolers at intervals. The teacher does not wait until the end of the story to begin the discussion. He/she would miss a number of queries because preschoolers could forget what they wanted to ask by the time the story is over. There should be natural pauses in the reading of the story so that youngsters can ask questions or make comments concerning the events in their lives that might relate to the story. Once this routine is established, the children will learn to expect the times when they can offer their input into the story-time event.

Children may *draw* a favorite character as part of the literacy routine, or *make a book* to include the drawing as a favorite literacy activity. *Role-playing* about the story may also be a part of the routine. Some youngsters are so exuberant about the role-playing activity that they have to be gently reminded that their peers must have a chance to express their thoughts as well. The reminder itself is a learning experience because preschoolers are *egocentric* and would not usually consider it odd to be the *center* of all discussions.

Another aspect of emerging literacy in preschoolers is the ability of the young child to *express himself/herself* orally so that meaning is conveyed to another person. Snow (1983) described oral language as "forms of communication, speaking, and listening" (p. 166). The following example was used in another chapter, and is relevant here as well. When Edward, who is in the block area, says to Joel, "You can play with me," Joel is happy and enters the block area to play. Joel proceeds to put a block on Edward's tower, but Edward yells, "Stop it." Joel is confused and replies, "But you said I can play with you." "Yeah, but I meant you could build your own stuff with the blocks; don't put blocks on my thing," said Edward. Thus, the concepts of *self-expression* and emerging literacy are interconnected in that the preschooler learns to both listen well and speak with clarity and focus. This is a learning process that takes time and patience. Miscommunication occurs daily with adults as well as with children.

Preschoolers are also learning that the spoken words which one hears can be encoded to appear at the bottom of the picture on the storybook page. *The squiggly lines on the bottom of the page are the spoken words that Mommy and the teacher read to me,* is the connection parents and educators want the child to gradually internalize.

The home is usually where youngsters receive their primary vocabulary and word meanings as conversations informally and naturally occur. But does the child really understand the complete meaning of the vocabulary used in conversation? According to Garton and Pratt (1989), children rely on the *context* of what is said to them as much as they rely on the

words themselves. "They understand key words and phrases . . . by rely-
ing heavily on the context to try to work out what is being said to them,
often subsequently producing errors of interpretation" (p. 102). For instance, a mother told her child to close the screen door so the flies would
not get into the house and bring germs. In a conversation later on with
another person, the child explained that germs were things that flies play
with (Garton & Pratt). Conversations that youngsters have with other
people can enhance the development of self-expression. The developmental process that fosters self-expression is dependent largely upon oral
communication between the youngster and a peer or a more knowledgeable person who will mediate that communication. Carrasquillo (1994)
said:

> Conversation is simply talking together about something of mutual interest. Effec-
> tive conversation requires: (a) using language others can understand, (b) using an
> appropriate tone of voice, (c) expressing ideas and responses clearly, (d) listening
> to others and (e) being aware of the body and facial cues of oneself and of others.
> (p. 135)

This type of oral activity occurs naturally in the home among family
members on a daily basis. In the home environment the child can receive
the one-to-one attention that focuses specifically on the topic, thereby
clarifying the content of the conversation and helping to clarify the vocabulary meaning.

It is also a part of the preschool curriculum to foster conversations and
discussions during a number of interactive situations. But the conversations and discussions are necessarily *not* one-to-one between adults and
children for any extended period, due to there being *many* children to
few adults in the classroom. Therefore, it is possible that less actual clarification of vocabulary is offered in a preschool environment as compared
to the home environment. Examples of times when conversations are not
one-to-one would be in the following areas: (a) during group circle meetings, where the plans of the day are discussed between the teacher and
the preschoolers, (b) during story-time circle, where the children listen to
and discuss the big book story, (c) during role-play activity, where the
youngsters can express the characters' monologue using the preschoolers'
own vocabulary, and (d) during free play. Talking and listening are involved in literally *every* aspect of the preschool daily routine, but *talking
and listening* among adults and children may not be as individualized for
each child as conversing at home. However, just because the activity is
not one-to-one doesn't necessarily mean literacy isn't occurring.

Fostering Language in Preschool

The teacher's role is that of mediator, guide, and enhancer of language as the *teachable moments* present themselves in preschool. For example, a preschooler told the teacher, "I wanna pee." The teacher responded, "You may use the lavatory." Many preschoolers in that class were saying, "I wanna use the labatory [*sic*]," by the end of the school year. Mediation is a type of restructuring of the preschoolers' vocabulary in a guiding manner, and in an unobtrusive context. This helps add to vocabulary and syntax in a teachable moment without formal structure in preschool settings. Another example is offered by Martinez (1997): "Look, her clothes rhyme. . . . Yes, her clothes match" (p. 70). The adult used the appropriate verb choice that fit into the child's thought without formal instruction and without changing the child's meaning in the sentence. Miller (1995) said, "Now that preschoolers are rapidly adding new words to their vocabulary, instead of using the term 'potty,' ask, 'Would you like to go to the toilet?' " (p. 46). Miller's example is yet another in the restructuring of vocabulary in an unobtrusive manner.

The use of unflattering remarks by the teacher to the child is never an acceptable way to teach any person anything. It could be devastating to a youngster to be told his/her vocabulary is inadequate. Carrasquillo (1994) noted that "the best way in which adults can help young language learners is by giving them guidance and encouragement" (p. 10). Guidance, attention, and encouragement are very effective incentives for preschoolers because they are still at an age where pleasing the adults in their lives is important to them. This may be an extension of pleasing their parents. Youngsters desire to please their parents because of the secure attachment that developed during infancy. If a secure attachment was not developed in infancy, there could be reasons for problems in interpersonal relationships later in life that may require intervention (Ainsworth, 1979).

Language skills begin to develop in terms of coherent formation of ideas based on experiences of many types. This means that the ideas come first in the youngster's mind; the ability to articulate those ideas comes second. These ideas are usually coherent inside the head of the youngster. The job for the young speaker is to be able to verbally express those ideas. "No one would deny that language development can be understood only as an aspect of the development of communication in general, and only in the context of the child's interactions" (Snow, 1983, p. 167). This quote appears to say that the context (situation, experiences) where the child's interactions are occurring fosters language development, and the communication of language to others. Therefore, numerous and varied contexts would enrich and add stimulation to development and enhancement of language acquisition, hence literacy.

Young students are constantly acquiring more attributes to map onto the words and phrases they use. As an example, some preschoolers refer to all toys with four wheels as *cars*, until they learn that there are trucks and vans with four wheels also on the toy shelf. Carrasquiilo (1994) said, "Long after children use a word or phrase, they are still acquiring attributes and experiencing the meaning of that word or phrase. The acquisition of meanings and concepts is a process that continues well beyond the early years" (p. 11).

As the young child's language develops, it need not be expressed in full sentences in order for meaning to be transferred from the youngster to the other person; the phrases of very young children will get the desired meaning across in almost all cases. According to Carrasquillo (1994), there is a stage called *early production* of language in which youngsters have a considerable understanding of some aspects of language and can use single words and phrases to convey their desires. This is a type of *telegraphic speech* in which only the essential words are spoken. "Want water," is full of meaning when coming from a 2-year-old child. The 4-year-old preschooler is using more words and fuller sentences. "I want a orange [sic]," one 4-year-old girl responded when asked whether she wanted orange juice or an orange for snack-time dessert in preschool.

Vocabulary building and syntax structure are occurring rapidly during preschool years in terms of the youngster expressing his/her ideas to a larger number of people than would be available to him/her at home. It is also occurring through the give-and-take responses of verbal communication with more knowledgeable people than himself/herself. This is in keeping with the Vygotskian theory of a *tutor* helping a *learner* to build on previous knowledge so that the learner becomes independent in doing the required work or class lessons on a more advanced level. This advancement is accomplished through the guided instruction of the tutor. Berg (1994) noted that "communication, expression, and reasoning are all developed through conversation, since it requires active processing of language with each participant's contribution contingent upon the others in an orderly sequence" (p. 39). It is the *reasoning* and *discussing* of information, whether during formal, direct instruction *or* informal, teachable moments, that lends itself to the guided tutoring so the learner can be helped by the tutor to progress to a higher level.

Literacy Acquisition and Themes

Berg (1994) further found that "literacy activities are best developed if the teacher places materials on a specific theme with each activity center in the room" (p. 39). It has been this writer's observation that when a writing center was thematic and the teacher had provided a general motif to guide the young students' imagination to a specific topic, say Thanksgiving or autumn, the youngsters responded with numerous *literacy behaviors*. Motifs refer to items on bulletin boards, displays of real pumpkins, real leaves, and real scarves and mittens. The following are some of the activities (literacy behaviors) that the children engaged in: (a) pretending to write on the bottom of their drawings, (b) engaging in explaining their stories to a peer as it related to their art work, (c) making book covers with a large picture and large pretend words for the book title, (d) and putting pretend-numbers on the bottom of the pages in the books. The children got these ideas about bookmaking from having had a relationship with books in the home and/or in preschool. The literacy behaviors were produced in a more prolific manner when the motifs were in place than when the writing center just had pens, pencils, papers, markers, etc.

Perhaps the motifs were instrumental in activating the youngsters' cognitive processes. For example, the pumpkin patches and turkeys were plentiful, with pretend writing on the bottom. Children engaged in storytelling, where peers sat together explaining their artwork to each other, and pretended to read. These types of literacy activities were seen much more often where peers sat in dyads or small groups and pretended to read their stories to the audience. Rybczynski and Troy (1995) stated, "Play centers offer rich opportunities for oral language development, as the children imitate language and refine their understanding of adult forms, vocabulary and conversational turn-taking" (p.7).

The same *materials* were out at the writing center during a 2-week span of time, but the *motifs* were absent when an *informal* experiment was conducted over a two week period in a preschool in the Bronx, New York. Data were collected *by observation* daily. The data consisted of ticking off on a checklist the number of drawings the children made *without* pretend writings on the bottom, drawings made *with* pretend writings on the bottom, books made by students, and conversations concerning books made by students.

The columns of the checklist were tallied daily for the two weeks. During the first week, *the motifs were present*, along with the materials, and the second week *there were no motifs*. More prolific literary behaviors occurred when the motif was in place. This is not offered as scientific data. There were no formal controls, just an informal display of motifs during the first week and no motifs the next week, with observations and comparisons of the literacy behaviors being made. This type of informal observation is an interesting and easy way for parents and teachers to compare different types of events.

Expansion of Literacy Through Storying

A second component of literacy acquisition is expanding previous knowledge through a form of conversation called *storying* (Canizares, 1997). This is a type of narrative that flows like a story, which includes more than just an accumulation of facts. Canizares said:

> What we're talking about here is constructing stories in the mind to process experiences—often referred to as storying. . . . Everyday conversation is filled with stories. By being immersed in this continuous exchange, children learn not only how to build relationships, but also how to enrich their sense of self." (pp. 48, 50)

By retelling the plot of a story, the youngsters are involved in a literacy activity that is popular and serves the purpose of reinforcing *storybook structure*. Storybook structure usually has a specific introduction of characters, of the plot, of the problem, of the build-up to climax, and finally the climax. Daily readings seem to insure that youngsters at least begin to internalize the structure of storybooks. Once children learn the structure they can learn to tell their own stories with some semblance of sequence. Learning the strategy of sequencing is a long process. This strategy is still being learned or refined in second or third grades.

According to Soundy and Genisio (1994), research indicates that dramatic play as well as storytelling by the children themselves are necessary for children to reach optimal language and literacy development. "Children are now being asked to tell their own stories . . . and retellings of old favorites. Teachers incorporate children's experiential backgrounds when guiding children to verbalize stories" (p. 20).

Recess playtime provides an excellent opportunity for literacy to take place in the form of a running extemporaneous story. This occurred during conversations between the pretend store clerk and the customer, during the discussion between the pretend Daddy and Mommy, and during the examination the pretend doctor conducted with the pretend patient. In such an episode of play, this writer witnessed the *doctor* telling the *patient* to sit down in the chair and get "a oppenation [*sic*]." The doctor asked the patient, "What's da matta wit you?" He put the stethoscope to the chest of the patient and pretended to listen to his heart. The patient replied, "I'm sick." The doctor listened to the patient's chest again and asked a few more questions. Then he said, "Okay, you had the openation [*sic*]. Who else want a openation [*sic*]?" Other children were lined up to join in the fun of experiencing a visit to the doctor's office and engaging in the conversations the visit entails.

The following is another example of budding literacy acquisition. Preschoolers who are read to at home or in preschool are receiving *cognitive stimulation* that tends to lay the groundwork for the understanding of story structure, *story schemata* (which is usually the plot and background experiences of the character), construction of meaning, reflection on personal experience and prior knowledge as they relate to the story, and recollection of main ideas of the story (Lehr, 1990). Children's storybook content is synonymous with the term *children's literature* in this chapter. Snow (1983) said, "Book reading routines constitute occasions for vocabulary acquisition, for the acquisition of bookhandling skills, for the discovery of print, for the recognition of words, and for the development of a story scheme which could ultimately contribute to reading comprehension" (p. 177).

Storybook reading and discussion in preschool is a precursor to developing reading comprehension because the youngsters have time to discuss the story as it progresses, which helps them gain a working knowledge of at least some part of the plot, the characters, and the climax of the story. When children begin to acquire this knowledge from the daily routine of being read to, they are actively learning to listen for clues and specific statements about the story. Harms and Lettow (1996) offered:

> Interacting with a work, however, is generally not complete unless children can express and share, in different ways, the ideas generated by reading. Responses from classmates is an important component, as well. The teacher plays a critical role in facilitating the entire process. (p. 213)

The sharing of ideas generates responses from peers. Harms and Lettow said in the quote that this is one way preschoolers comprehend the essence of the story. When youngsters retell the story, they are learning the procedure that Canizares termed storying.

The internalization of particular parts of a story can be expressed as the preschooler retells the story. Interacting with a small group of peers facilitates this process. Antonacci (1994) noted that "the small-group discussion is suggested because its format encourages interaction by members who would find it difficult to speak to larger numbers" (p. 30). Members of that small group can fill in areas of the story that the reteller has omitted because those areas were not critical to the reteller, but were critical to other group members. In this small group learning experience, members are all rehearing elements that may have escaped them for various reasons the first time the story was read by the teacher. But they are now being refocused on those elements in the small group retelling and discussion activity in order to bring about expansion of cognition to each member. The group members do not realize that they are stimulating each other intellectually. That is an inevitable literacy by-product of the group's conversations.

Another component of literacy acquisition for preschoolers is the authentic drawings they do concerning the story being discussed in their small groups. Watch the children; learn to be an observer as well as a teacher. Youngsters become quite absorbed in the process of illustration. Some children will do a few lines and curves and call it their drawing. But you want to look for the serious artist, the children who are involved with the paper and markers or crayons. These children are producing thoughts and processing ideas.

Later, the teacher will write the caption for the pictures as preschoolers dictate the sentences. Or the preschoolers themselves may put pretend-writing on the bottom of their drawings as captions. All of these activities are literacy behaviors. The drawings are either hung up in the classroom or put together to form a class-book. This is affirmation and publication of the child's emerging literacy ability to comprehend written material for recall of detail as well as global meaning, which is a crucial skill for later success in school. Kantor, Miller, and Fernie (1992) found in their study that:

> Within the supportive environment of the writing and art tables and through dialogue, children in this study learned the roles of author and audience, confronted new ideas and conflicts about print construction and meaning, and expanded their literacy knowledge. (p. 187)

As the person reading the story stops at critical points to discuss the characters, plot, and setting of the story with the youngsters, they are reflecting on the cause-and-effect aspect of the events of the story. This is one component of story structure. For instance, three bears went for a walk into the woods because they had a *problem*. The problem needed a solution. The problem was that the porridge for their breakfast was far too hot for the bears to eat. The *solution* was that the bear family could go into the woods for a walk, allowing the *porridge to cool* in their absence.

Problem and solution are sophisticated concepts, which can be broken down into discussions that are relevant to the preschooler's life. These discussions can be small episodes that logically connect the sequence of events that pertain to the *why* of the problem. To illustrate, when a youngster's mother cooks cereal at home, the cereal gets very hot. This is the connection that the child can be helped to make between the story about bears and real life. The solution in the story is that the three bears can go into the woods for a walk while the porridge cools. The solution at home is that the youngster has to either wait for the cereal to cool, or blow it cool by mouth before eating it.

Construction of Meaning

Construction of meaning and reflection on personal experience are integral parts of understanding what the main idea of the story is. When a youngster can relate the events in the book specifically to his/her personal life, this indicates that a connection has begun to form between events in the storybook (literature) and comprehension of the genre, termed *story.* Lehr (1990) said "the ability to identify themes seems to develop earlier than theme generation, and requires at least a general level of awareness of the meaning of the story" (p. 38). The general identification of theme, which is global, seems to occur about the same time as the construction of meaning of the story. For instance, when a preschooler was listening to a story about a bicycle, she wanted to talk about her sister's bike:

> It was important for Meg to share that story about her sister's bike becoming smashed by her mom's car. Reading is interactive. Young children must be given the opportunity to share what they know during book events and those book experiences will frequently trigger information that the child links to life experiences. (Lehr, 1990, p. 42)

The linking of story events to life experiences is an interactive process that may be a precursor to the development of crucial reading comprehension skills for success in elementary school and beyond (Katz and Chard, 1991).

Recalling the main idea of a story is another way that the youngster can interact with the story text. Each member of the three bears' family had a specific bowl, a chair, and a bed that each bear family member could call his/her own personal property. A youngster may be able to relate to this in terms of the egocentric stage that Piaget places the child in between the ages of 2- and 7-years-old. That is to say, youngsters relish having things that are totally theirs. So, when Goldilocks eats, sits, and sleeps in the bears' personal property, preschoolers may be able to empathize with the three bears' problem.

Some youngsters may need more time to experience story-time circle in order *to develop the sense of plot and theme (schemata).* Lehr (1990) found in her study that "only one of the children, generally speaking, was able to locate the central components of the story" (p. 41). This idea of *recalling the main* idea may also take more time to develop for some young students. With recurring dialogue concerning what has been read and its relevancy to the youngster, the child who needs more time to locate central components of the story will gradually catch on. As long as the ideas in the story have some relevancy in the child's mind that he/she can make a connection to in his/her life's experience, the child can begin to comprehend the story. "He simply offered some information about himself in response to the specific question about the most important idea in the story. He generalized the story and made a mesh with his own perceptions" (Lehr, 1990, p. 43). Whatever the information about himself was, in the Lehr quote, the adult wisely accepted his perceptions. It told the adult that the boy understood the theme, even if on a rudimentary level.

Re-Reading Stories

Do youngsters get bored by hearing the same stories read to them over and again? Generally speaking, no. Youngsters relish this procedure because it allows them to 'predict' the outcome of the story successfully, every time! They already know the outcome of events due to having heard the same story previously. But when youngsters can say, in advance, what will occur in the story, they may feel in control of the event and subsequently, feel powerful. The task of prediction is *concrete* in the sense of having been rehearsed in previous readings, so that youngsters know their predictions of the story are always correct. And youngsters begin to realize the story will always relate to their lives in the same way as it did in previous readings. This is the *constancy of the printed page.*

Children can always rely on what the book will say. When the teacher or parent attempts to paraphrase the story line, perhaps to shorten the book-reading session, the child has been known to say, "Oh no! That's not what the wolf said."

When the child begins to become familiar with literacy and begins to experience *literacy situations*, the youngster internalizes a sense of comfort from being able to rely on words in the book to always say what they said previously. And, the pictures are there every time he/she opens the book, no matter how many times! This sense of comfort *can prompt a youngster's creative and imaginative processes into action*. When the opportunity presents itself, the child can begin to *embellish* an event that actually occurred. Example at hand, this writer overheard a group of three youngsters in the play-yard discussing how a small spider and an ant were friends because they both came crawling from the same general direction across the play-yard rubber matting. As the three preschoolers discussed this friendship between spider and ant, details *creatively advanced* to where the spider and ant were said to have babies that played together under the steps. All of this creative cognition spontaneously occurred at recess because three preschoolers became aware of a small spider and an ant as they came out from under the steps and scurried across the rubber matting. These youngsters were exhibiting story structure.

Developing Higher Level Cognition During Story-Time Circle

The story-time circle in preschool is a time for group interaction by engaging in the following routine: (a) the teacher introducing the story, (b) reminding students of listening skills, (c) discussing some aspects of the story with the class, (d) predicting some story outcomes with the class, (e) discussing how the story relates to the students' personal life, and then (f) reading the story to the class. After the story has been read, it will be discussed *again*. There are seven steps listed in the process of reading a story. Are they all necessary to have a successful reading and comprehension session in story-time circle? Probably not. However, the preparatory steps of *introducing the story, relating the essence of the story to students' lives, reading the story, and then discussing the story* in reference to the students' lives is valued as a basic routine that should be done so that it gives the youngsters a good introduction and lead-in to enjoying, interacting, and comprehending the story. It also helps the youngsters to somewhat solidify the content in their minds after the story has been read to them.

The teacher proceeds to ask questions of the children that relate to that day's story. By opening the discussion with personal events from the children's lives and predicting outcome, the teacher uses the "prereading strategy of asking students to predict" possible outcomes of the story (Elfant, 1994, p. 142). This strategy is "an effective instructional method that facilitates access to prior knowledge" (p. 142). Predictions about the present story may foster retrieval of prior knowledge of either real events or previous storybook events. The retrieval of prior knowledge is a higher-level cognitive process. Interaction between the story and prior life's experience tends to make the story more meaningful to the child. He/she can become more emotionally and intellectually involved in the reading event.

Next, youngsters listen to the teacher read the big-book story. However, *listening quietly* is not the critical component of being read to. *Interaction* between teacher and youngsters, and youngsters and story line are critical components for the following reasons: (a) each youngster hears the story and sees the pictures in the book, (b) each youngster potentially begins to realize that the print on the page always says the same thing every time that particular book is read, (c) each youngster potentially begins to make connections between the content of the book and some similar event in his/her personal life, and (d) each youngster may begin to feel a desire to express his/her thoughts in terms of some aspect of the story as he/she interacts cognitively with the story. *The reading event becomes a personal event to each child in a different and specific way.*

There is a level of security and comfort in the predictable procedure of the story-time circle. The fact that story-time circle is a social experience that engages youngsters' minds and involves them in the events occurring on the pages is an expansion of the children's minds. It is a higher-level process that can help to ready the children for *intrapsychological* interpretations of what the children are hearing and discussing.

Vygotsky and the Storybook

The intrapsychological interpretation is a Vygotskian theory which relates to the rethinking of the social learning interactions and experiences which have occurred during the youngster's day. These experiences are expressed in *inner speech,* which occurs as a mental process in the youngster as he/she revisits the social and learning experiences. The process allows for cognitive interactions and interpretations of those previous experiences so that the young student goes through a process of sorting out the events and experiences to make sense of them. *The child talks to himself/herself inside his/her head,* as it were. Developmental cognition is in the process of taking place. Teale and Sulzby (1986) stated, "For Vygotsky the foundations of cognition are social in nature. He proposed that individuals' higher psychological processes . . . were reflections of social processes in which they participated at earlier points in their development" (p. 113).

When necessary, a process termed *scaffolding* (a Bruner term), is employed, through which the youngster is helped to reach a higher level of understanding of the events which occurred throughout the day. This is done with the help of a more knowledgeable person (peer or adult) in the form of tutoring. The tutoring takes place in what Vygotsky termed the *zone of proximal development* (*ZPD*). This zone is an expanse of mental area which consists of a beginning level of knowledge on which the preschooler can function. The tutor helps the preschooler reach a higher level of knowledge by helping him/her internalize new material, which is added knowledge.

The internalization of new material and making sense of it is what Piaget termed *assimilation of new information with previously acquired information.* The youngster has been helped or enriched by a more knowledgeable tutor to the higher level where the youngster can now function independently. He/she previously could not function on this higher level. "Vygotsky found that instruction precedes development and that the learner can learn some aspects of cognition through demonstration and experience" (Hedley, 1994, p. 10). Instruction preceding the development is "an example of Vygotsky's notion that teaching should always be in advance of development" (Teale & Sulzby, 1986, p. 126). This means that the preschool youngster *first has to have social experiences and interactions with peers and with the environment so that development in social and cognitive domains can be enhanced as these domains develop.* The youngster is then ready for the next phase.

The next phase, which occurs immediately after the experiences and interactions take place, is the *intrapsychological process.* This means the youngster begins to ruminate over the experiences and social interactions to concretize them mentally. Then, a more knowledgeable tutor can help the youngster further develop the material that he/she may have been experiencing trouble sorting through. After the tutoring sessions, when the youngster is functioning at a higher level, he/she is said to be at an *independent level* of cognition of the assimilated old and new knowledge.

In Summary

Literacy knowledge that some youngsters *bring with them* into preschool can be the underpinnings of interactions with story-time circle experiences. Youngsters who have been exposed to a routine of being read to regularly have begun to realize that "the print not the picture contains the story that is being read," and the youngsters "are able to locate a word" (Teale & Sulzby, 1986, p. 115). Youngsters who enter preschool with this background knowledge seem to have a giant head-start over the youngsters who have to first realize that the black marks at the bottom of the page (the print) will always say the same thing each time the teacher reads that particular storybook. This writer remembers reading Goldilocks and the Three Bears to preschoolers and having one youngster ask if the bears will ever catch the girl as she runs away at the end of the story? This showed the preschooler's ability to ask an intelligent and thoughtful question. It also revealed that he was just beginning to become familiar with the constancy of printed words.

It is vital that parents and preschool educators capitalize on the rich, fertile minds of youngsters who are eager to absorb new experiences from infancy through the age of five. These years are a time when access to storybooks, to conversations, and mediation of language expression by adults all help greatly in introducing and sustaining early literacy to the preschooler. "Although storybook reading is most often an activity not engaged in for the express purpose of deliberately teaching young children to read, it plays a key role in the process of becoming literate" (Teale & Sulzby, 1986, p. 127).

References

Ainsworth, M. D. S. (1979). Infant-mother attachment. *The American Psychological Association, 34*(10), 932–937.

Antonacci, P. A. (1994). Oral language development. In P. Antonacci & C. N. Hedley (Eds.), *Natural approaches to reading and writing* (pp. 19–32). Norwood, NJ: Ablex.

Berg, D. N. (1994). The role of play in literacy development. In P. Antonacci & C. N. Hedley (Eds.), *Natural approaches to reading and writing* (pp. 34–48). Norwood, NJ: Ablex.

Canizares, S. (1997). Sharing stories. *Early Childhood Today, 12*(3), 47, 48, 50, 52.

Carrasquillo, A. L. (1994). *Teaching English as a second language.* New York: Garland Publishing, Inc.

Elfant, P. C. (1994). He's not looking at the book! Metacognition and the young child. In P. Antonacci & C. N. Hedley (Eds.), *Natural approaches to reading and writing* (pp. 142–154). Norwood, NJ: Ablex.

Fox, S. (1997). The controversy over ebonics. *Phi Delta Kappan, 79*(3), 237–240.

Harms, J. M., & Lettow, L. J. (1996). Interacting with inner audiences to extend reading experiences. *Childhood Education, 72*(4), 210–213.

Hedley, C. N. (1994). Theories of natural language. In P. Antonacci & C. N. Hedley (Eds.), *Natural approaches to reading and writing* (pp. 3–18). Norwood, NJ: Ablex.

Kantor, R., Miller, M. M., & Fernie, D. E. (1992). Diverse paths to literacy in a preschool classroom: A sociocultural perspective. *Reading Research Quarterly, 27*(3), 185–201.

Katz, L. G., & Chard, S. C. (1991). *Engaging children's minds: The project approach.* Norwood, NJ: Ablex.

Lehr, S. (1990). Literature and the construction of meaning: The preschool child's developing sense of theme. *Journal of Research in Childhood Education, 5*(1), 37–46.

Martinez, M. (1997). Young children as explorers of language. *Early Childhood Today, 12*(3), 69–71.

Miller, S. A. (1995). Bathroom talk. *Early Childhood Today, 9*(5), 46.

Rybczynski, M., & Troy, A. (1995). Literacy-enriched play centers: Trying them out in the real world. *Childhood Education, 72*(1), 7–12.

Sigel, I. E. (1993). Educating the young thinker: A distancing model of preschool education. In J. L. Roopnarine & J. E. Johnson (Eds.), *Approaches to early childhood education* (pp. 179–194). New York: Macmillan Publishers.

Snow, C. E. (1983). Literacy and language: Relationships during the preschool years. *Harvard Educational Review, 53*(2), 165–189.

Soundy, C. S., & Genisio, M. H. (1994). Asking young children to tell the story. *Childhood Education, 71*(1), 20–23.

Teale, W. H., & Sulzby, E. (1986). *Emergent literacy: Writing and reading.* Norwood, NJ: Ablex.

York, L. (1995). Supporting at-home literacy. *Early Childhood Today, 9*(8), 30, 35.

Chapter 6

Preschoolers in the Block Area

Plastic and wooden building blocks are a part of the collection of toys in many homes. Youngsters from these homes are familiar with the attributes of these toys. Their parents realized, in the years before their children entered preschool, the benefits of the children stacking the blocks, knocking them down, and placing them end to end on the floor. These games entertained each youngster, but they were much more than entertainment. The games introduced the child to the idea that objects placed on top of one another can fall down if they are pushed. The objects never fall up. Blocks placed end to end on the floor eventually reach from here to way over there. True, the child does not consciously form these thoughts while playing with the blocks. But this background knowledge is stored for later use and understanding.

Preschoolers may have made structures in the home and *named* those structures after things they are familiar with (Segal & Adcock, 1986). For example, a stack of blocks could be named "our church" by the young child. Some children may not have reached the stage of naming block structures. Naming the structure involves moving into a more sophisticated area of awareness. If a child has reached that level at home, before entering preschool, perhaps it is because the parents have asked on a number of occasions, "What is this you have made?" In that example, the child may have internalized that the block structures can represent objects he/she sees in life. But the child may not want to name his/her structures. It is okay if the structure has no name. Adults need not insist on a name. The child may become confused if he/she is forced to name the structures because for him/her the delight and satisfaction comes from creating, not necessarily naming. The youngster may be at the beginning stage of physical and concrete discovery and not yet ready to have the structures become symbolic for him/her.

The obvious role of blocks in preschool would be to provide the young-ster with building material for constructing such things as towers, roads, and tall buildings. Blocks fill those functions, but they contribute so much more. Playing with blocks can be an experience that fosters creative and imaginative thought processes. For instance, when a youngster plays in the kitchen area, the stove, table, and refrigerator are entities that have specific designations. But blocks have the unique distinction of becoming all the things that the child's imagination can create. "Block projects can span long periods of time—and can be as extensive and detailed as children's interest and curiosity allow" (Weiss, 1997, p. 32). Castles, boats, and hospitals are no problem for the youngster to build. Then his/her imagination supplies the verbal script in solitary play, or with peers.

The block area is filled with blocks of wood and plastic; they are large, medium, and small specimens. Some of the plastic blocks are red, blue, yellow, and green. These attributes can be useful if youngsters are sorting or categorizing blocks or creating patterns. Why do preschoolers find block-building so fascinating? How do they use the blocks, to make tall structures that reach upward, or those structures that spread out to take up floor space? This chapter offers some insight into these questions.

Playing with Blocks as a Cooperative Effort

The block area offers a "physical context for children to experience coop-eration, collaboration, and dialogue. . . . Children are involved in making decisions and solving problems that affect the outcome of their play" (Drew, 1997, p. 40). Youngsters working on a project *together* must make *collaborative decisions* about the physical arrangement of the struc-ture they are building. This collaboration is a learning experience that is not easy for preschoolers because they are in what Piaget called the *ego-centric stage*. This is the stage where each child is self-centered and very sure that *his/her* idea is the only one that has relevance to the project. Sometimes there will be yelling and pouting in the block area as the children attempt to negotiate the terms of constructing the project. These disagreements create interactive tension and/or creative tension as the students learn to work through their problems and come to terms with each other.

Preschoolers working in the block area are beginning to use their ideas to enhance skills that can relate to situations in later life. To illustrate, a parent putting the groceries away in the kitchen cabinet at home has to arrange the cans so that they fit into the limited space on the shelf.

Preschoolers working with blocks come to realize, by trial and error at first, just how many blocks it takes to make a 'rug' fit into the designated area. A rug is an expanse of blocks put down on the floor edge-to-edge and end-to-end. Otherwise, the rug will wind up intruding into the library area floor space. Moffitt (1974) noted, "Some children tend to build very compactly while others tend to extend their structures. Children learn that there are certain conditions and limitations in space" (p. 29).

Learning to use space economically in the block area can only be initially accomplished by trial and error. After the blocks have actually been placed on the floor, preschoolers begin to visually and physically realize that not even one more block can fit in a particular space. These early mathematical concepts cannot be explained to preschoolers. They have to be experienced daily by youngsters in the block area.

"When preschool children . . . build they are learning about spatial relations, how to arrange and combine elements so that the whole is recognizable and pleasing to look at" (Segal & Adcock, 1986, p. 100). Blocks can stretch the imagination of youngsters because the wooden and plastic attributes of the blocks and their short or long attributes offer an expanse of creative possibilities for children to explore. When children use blocks for construction of anything from roads to towers, they are conceptualizing the use of space, distance, direction, and patterns. "Each block has certain qualities such as size, shape, and weight. . . . Children soon learn to differentiate many of these dimensions" (Moffitt, 1974, p. 25). It was found to be an asset to include "the use of blocks as a medium of expression . . . of the ideas and feelings expressed by children from two-to-six-years-of-age" (Moffitt, 1974, p. 10). The quote suggests that when children have ideas about anything from racing cars to baking cakes, they can express those ideas with blocks. Blocks can become the road on which to drive the pretend car, and a block can also become the car itself. Blocks can become an airplane that is an enclosed structure for a child to sit inside. The child can pretend to be going on a trip to see Grandma because he/she misses Grandma very much.

Stages of Construction Using Blocks

According to Moffitt (1974), there are specific stages of building structures that youngsters employ when playing with blocks. The *first stage* is that "blocks are carried from place to place, or they may be stacked" (Moffitt, p. 10). This procedure is usually carried out by children between 2-to-3-years-old. It appears to be an empowering activity for youngsters because the blocks go wherever the child wants them to go. After children get used to the feel and weight of the blocks, they may begin to place blocks on top of one another to form towers. They also may place blocks side by side. Some builders place blocks edge to edge to create what appears to be a mat or a rug. Segal and Adcock (1986) observed that "a flat line of blocks can be reproduced again and again until the line has become a rectangular platform or floor" (p. 95). Youngsters may even walk across the mat, rug, or floor they have created, thereby giving credence to its existence as a floor.

This type of activity is repeated over again until the child either decides to elaborate on the structure or move on to the next stage in block building. In concurrence with Moffitt, Brody (1974) found that the first block structures in preschool were:

> Usually blocks . . . placed horizontally one next to the other. They are generally of the same size. This configuration appears to be a road, a train, or a track to the adult. In the child's fantasy, the block formation may be something entirely different. (p. 59)

The *second stage* is usually the wall, bridge, and fence structures. Moffitt (1974) said, "These are fairly predictable stages in the building activities" (p. 13). These structures are produced and repeated just as the towers and mats were repeatedly built. After satiation with bridges and fences, the next stage emerges.

This *third stage* is often the enclosed structure. For instance, the prince builds walls where he can go inside his castle and command his guards to bring him things. The captain can build his ship and sail away. The mom can go inside the house she has built and invite friends over to have a conversation with her. "Another insight is that internal space can be embellished with objects. Younger preschool children fill their pens with animals and cars" (Segal & Adcock, 1986, p. 96). Dolls and dishes may be brought into the block enclosure to further enhance the fantasy. In this way creativity can be displayed, and imagination is fostered. The richness and diversity of the youngster's language is also fostered in this situation.

These first three stages generally are exhibited in this order; however, Moffitt (1974) stated that the degree or length of time each student spends in a particular stage could vary:

> When a child is once able to see blocks as building material which is capable of being put together in an ordered arrangement, a variety of methods, patterns, and techniques seem to suggest themselves to him. With age, there is a steady

increase in facility, imagination, elaboration of design, and actual number of blocks used. (p. 16)

The *fourth stage* tends to be 'patterning.' This means that a youngster will generally place a block with a specific shape on the floor or table, followed by a specific block of another shape or color. There are now two blocks on the floor. The next block will be the same as the first, and the fourth block will be the same as the second. In this example, a pattern is emerging. This activity can be performed by a single child or a group of children. Moffitt (1974) offered:

> As he builds, he learns that there are certain sequential patterns that need to be followed when he places different blocks in relationship to one another. Children tend to develop a variety of sequential patterns, which they repeat over and over again. (p. 26)

The building activity may progress to include a partner who can be permanently engaged in the activity until the structure is complete, or who moves in and out of the building episode. Youngsters "create and recognize patterns . . . and solve problems in the physical domain. Children experiment with various patterns of blocks and make hypotheses regarding balance, symmetry, weight, and force" (Weiss, 1997, p. 37). Later, there may be clusters or groups of children working in proximity, but not on the same building project. This is termed *parallel block play*. It becomes *associative block play* if there is at least minimal interaction between peers while building their structures.

The *fifth and final stage* is when youngsters work together in a group on the same project, but on different aspects of it. This fifth stage is true interaction and involvement with other peers. Planning, in terms of what the structure is turning out to be, is also involved in this final stage. Wilford (1996) said:

> In working together to create a complex structure out of blocks, children are practicing science skills such as hypothesizing, estimating weight, and exploring balance. They are also learning social skills such as negotiation and compromise. But beyond these skills lies the impulse to create, a desire to make something pleasing. First comes the concept. After a process of discussion and compromise, a structure is created that is acceptable to the whole group. (p. 33)

What a complex, involved, and sophisticated learning progression from playing with blocks at home, before entering preschool, to creating structures with peers that are acceptable to all members of the group. This process is not quick, nor is it easy. Most preschoolers proceed through these five stages of block building. As Moffitt (1974) suggested, the process is sequential, but does not necessarily take the same span of time to accomplish from child to child. The process should not be hurried. Each youngster takes the time he/she needs, as an individual, to pass through the stages.

Becoming the Created Structure

Some youngsters can get so involved and absorbed in their fantasy that they actually *become* the objects they are in the process of creating. For example, Tom has made a boat enclosure where he sits inside and makes the sound of the boat as it moves in the water, "Chugga, chugga, chugga." None of the other preschoolers find this behavior odd because they understand the experience he is having at the moment. They, too, have those experiences when they give themselves over to imagination. The child who has chosen to be the family pet says, "Ruff, ruff" because he/she has become the puppy. The child also makes the movements of the puppy by wagging his/her imaginary tail and using her hands as paws. All of this connotes intelligence and inference based on what the child has previously seen puppies do, or what he/she has heard or read about puppies.

The internal idea of a boat on the lake becomes a reality for Tom when he builds the structure. But when he also makes the sounds that he has heard boats make on the lake, Tom becomes a boat in the same way that Mary becomes a princess when she puts on the tiara from the dress-up box of clothes in the housekeeping area. As with the child who became the puppy, these creative and imaginative expeditions by children into themselves can help ready them for a deeper understanding of what they will later encounter in their school careers. Rogers and Sawyers (1988) offered:

> Denise is a watch dog. She hides behinds a cabinet, then pounces out to scare her teacher, barking "Woof! Woof!" Sabastian is a train. "Here comes the train," he announces, Whooo, Whooo, watch out or I will run over you!" Children can pretend to be other people, animals, or even things. They begin with a single scheme, and imitate increasingly complex behaviors and characteristics. (p. 39)

In all these cases, the imagination causes thought processes to continue stretching and expanding to include new monologue, or dialogue if the youngster becomes a second person or thing while involved in his/her fantasy. "Once the child moves into using a symbolic self . . . he or she may alternately be mother, baby, father, teacher (Cuffaro, 1974, p. 17–18). This appears to be an empowering process that allows the youngster to have control over what he/she is too small to otherwise control. It seems to be a part of the imaginary independence the child wants to have but is really too fearful to think about the experiences in reality. Children can use fantasy for adventure and still have Mom and Dad in reality for safety and protection.

In Summary

Blocks are a mainstay in the preschool curriculum because they help the youngsters express themselves in varied ways. Blocks encourage mathematical concepts through the hands-on approach that concretizes the experiences for the children. Creativity and imagination are encouraged as the youngsters seem to mentally become the objects or people they imagine themselves to be in the block area. Sometimes this 'becoming' is an empowering experience for the preschooler who may use this opportunity to say or do something he/she would not dare do or say in 'real life.' Blocks, then, appear to serve a multidimensional role in the preschool.

References

Brody, C. (1974). Social studies and self-awareness. In E. S. Hirsh (Ed.), *The block book* (pp. 59–68). National Association for the Education of Young Children, Washington, DC.

Cuffaro, H. K. (1974). Dramatic play—the experience of block building. In E. S. Hirsh (Ed.), *The block book* (pp. 69–88). National Association for the Education of Young Children, Washington, DC.

Drew, W. (1997). Dr. Drew on his discovery blocks. *Early Childhood Today, 12*(2), 40–42.

Moffitt, M. W. (1974). Children learn about science through block building. In E. S. Hirsh (Ed.), *The block book* (pp. 25–32). National Association for the Education of Young Children, Washington, DC.

Rogers, C. S., & Sawyers, K. S. (1988). *Play in the lives of children.* National Association for the Education of Young Children, Washington, DC.

Segal, M., & Adcock, D. (1986). *Your child at play: Three to five years.* New York: Newmarket Press.

Weiss, K. (1997). Let's build. *Early Childhood Today, 12*(2), 30–39.

Wilford, S. (1996). Outdoor play. *Early Childhood Today, 10*(7), 31–36.

Chapter 7

Play and Sociodramatic Play in Preschool

According to Wilburn (1997), "the basic components of sociodramatic play appear to be *pretend characterization* and *real-life situations* in the child's prior knowledge base" (p. 8). Further, Berg (1994) offered this explanation and used it as a link to future reading: "Sociodramatic play, a form of symbolic play, has the clearest link to reading because it involves both simple and complex uses of imagination and through it a child manipulates reality and time" (p. 34). So, in Berg's explanation, sociodramatic play is a link to *academic skills*. Stone (1996) said, "In sociodramatic play, children transform simple objects into play tools. Children also take on fantasy roles . . ." (p. 105). However, the definition of *play*, according to Wilburn, is more lengthy and encompasses more situations than the definition of *sociodramatic play*. Wilburn (1997) described play as follows:

> Behaviors that are creative, voluntary, flexible, pleasurable, self-motivated, concerned more with means than ends (Berg, 1994; Goldhaber, 1994). Play also refers to the three types of play: solitary, parallel, and cooperative. Play is developmentally appropriate for preschoolers to provide a means of self-expression. This expression can incorporate roles and contexts the student has experienced previous to entering school. Play provides an avenue for novel interpretations and expansions of those experiences. (p. 25)

It is irrelevant whether a young child is exhibiting *play* or *sociodramatic play* as described in the quotes above. As long as play is ongoing and engaged in frequently by preschoolers, all types of play are immensely beneficial to the child.

Young children's play themes come to them from many sources. Youngsters naturally imitate the adults and circumstances that they see daily in their environment. But children are by no means limited to these realities for sources of themes to act out creatively. The fertile, impressionable, and creative imaginations of children will take them on journeys as far away as other planets or places as near as the next door neighbor's house. These journeys occur first in the children's heads—in their imaginations— then in their interactive play. Wallace (1995) suggested:

> There is nothing odd or novel about creative thinking. We all operate as a physical and biological cosmos and, therefore, innately own the vital change mechanism that functions as our creative process. Creative potential is a natural gift. (p. 34)

All of the journeys and dialogues that a child uses during play have to first take place in the imagination of the youngster. The captain of the ship says, "The sea is making the ship almost turn over, ahhha, ohhho! Everybody pick up the buckets and throw the water out, ahhha, ohhho." "Okay captain, we'll help. We'll save the ship." "Ohhho, we're sinking ohhho!" "I'll save you, captain." This scene took place in a preschool classroom. There were a number of characters involved in the pretend interaction between the captain and his crew on the ship. But *one* boy played all the parts. He was captain, and he was all the members of his own crew as well. "Once the child moves into using a symbolic self . . . he or she may alternately be mother, baby, father, teacher. . . ." (Cuffaro, 1974, p. 17).

"Playfulness in a learning context, deemphasizes the need to be perfect and, thus, increases children's self-esteem; therefore, it also increases children's willingness to develop interpersonal relationships through synergistic endeavors" (Boyer, 1997, p. 90). The *learning context* for the preschooler in Boyer's quote may be learning how to negotiate the role he/she wants to assume in the housekeeping area when a peer wants to play the same role, or learning how to retell a story in terms of story structure when pretending to be the teacher.

Play has a number of functions for children. Stone (1996) said, "As children play, they learn social skills such as how to negotiate, resolve conflicts, take turns, and share. Play opportunities help children develop friendships and provide a release from the stresses they face" (p. 104). During play the child has the opportunity to say or do what he/she was not able to express when a real-life situation was occurring. In this way, play opportunities can also function as coping mechanisms and empowering situations.

Through play youngsters begin to learn how to cope with situations and events in their lives that might have an overwhelming effect on them.

It may be difficult for a child to always have to do what adults tell him/her to do, so the child becomes the Mommy, through play, and tells others what to do. During morning recess, a peer ran real fast and arrived at the sliding board before anyone else. Charlene, another youngster, wanted to be first, and was unhappy. So during afternoon recess, Charlene became Supergirl, who could fly really, really fast over to the sliding board and be first any time she wanted.

Extend this behavior to the many characters a child portrays through the medium of play, and adults may gain some insight into what might be causing pleasure or pain in a youngster's life. Adults can begin to recognize which circumstances are uncomfortable for the youngster, which circumstances the child is sorting out successfully, and which he/she is having more difficulty in handling. Weller (1996) said about children, "Under the protection of play, they can expose emotions with a feeling of safety. The freedom to symbolize experiences through play provides them with an emotional safety valve that can help them live through defeats, frustrations, and pain" (Weller, 1996, CD, Compton's Interactive Encyclopedia). Brewer and Kieff (1997) stated, "Play helps children's emotional development. . . . They have opportunities to play out their fears and gain control of their anxieties" (p. 92).

Imagination (along with fantasy, pretense, and creativity are viewed as crossover concepts in this chapter) can be a conduit for play themes that children use that is far superior to adult imagination; adults may have become too limited by reality to engage in spontaneous frivolity. But youngsters are only limited to the extent of their abilities to fantasize and create situations. Hartle (1996) offered:

> Pretense activity has a number of developmental accomplishments, including providing a mechanism for alleviating anxieties and fears, fostering the development of self-confidence and self-regulation, promoting exploration of the environment or multiple uses of objects, promoting abstract thinking, stimulating language based on imagery, allowing for the practice and refinement of interactive rules, and helping children to reduce egocentricity by taking on the roles of others. (p. 68)

Stimulation is needed so children can have the background from which to begin their imaginary journeys. Youngsters go on trips, feel soft cookie dough, dig in dirt, go to see plays, eat in restaurants, listen to books being read to them, play in the park with peers, ride bicycles, and experience so much more as they grow from infancy into preschoolers. All of these varied experiences provide the background from which youngsters imagine and create their play situations. To illustrate, one does not usually become a captain of a ship with a crew if one has never heard stories about ships or seen films about such things. This is one reason that a rich and diverse background full of experiences and situations is crucial in the formative years of early childhood.

Youngsters learn while they play, through a process called *cognitive discrepancy*, according to Rogers and Sawyers (1988). This means that a child will take the play situation to a level where that child is comfortable, where he/she can make it mean something that is specific to him/her personally. Later, during the play episode, a situation may evolve where the youngster needs help in fulfilling his/her character-role. At that point, the youngster can seek the needed help in a way that is appropriate for him/her in the play situation. Rogers and Sawyers (1988) offered this example:

> Sheroka, who is a doctor, begins to fill out a prescription pad, writing Rx and numbers for the number of days her patient is to take the medicine. Another doctor, Robbie, comes to the teacher concerned that he does not know how to spell words on the prescription. (p. 2)

Both youngsters encountered cognitive discrepancy when their character-role needed something extra. In this case, knowledge of writing a prescription was needed. One child, Sheroka, thought that the Rx (prescription symbol) and numbers would be a good prescription. The other child, Robbie, thought that words were needed for his prescription but he did not know how to write them. He sought the teacher's help. Sheroka did not need another person's help. She was comfortable using her own method of writing the prescription. Sheroka resolved any cognitive discrepancy that may have momentarily arisen. Each child handled the cognitive discrepancy in the play experience in a way that was appropriate and comfortable for him/her.

Children moderate their play interactions by adjusting the level of simplicity and complexity according to their comfort zone. "The fantasy world of the children helps them to understand themselves and the world around them, but that understanding is at their own, not an adult's level" (Weller, 1996, CD, Compton's Interactive Encyclopedia). Consider the following dialogue between two boys in preschool: "Yeah, yeah, and make alieve [sic] that the monster came on the ship. Ohhhh, ohhh the monster is tryin' to eat me. Save me, Michael." "No, no, make alieve the monster ate you." "No! Don't let him eat me. You gotta save me!" "No, make alieve I jumped off the ship and he ate you." "No! He ain't eatin' me! Let him eat you!" These two boys were negotiating the terms of play. They were controlling the directional path of their play. One youngster wants the other peer to be eaten up by the monster. Why? "Play becomes a suitable outlet for expressing negative feelings, hostility, and aggression" (Gordon & Browne, 1989, p. 326).

It is interesting that one youngster wanted the monster to eat the other child in the dialogue above. Maybe he saw something like that in a film, or heard it in a story. Or, maybe he remembered that his peer had done something to him that he didn't like. Now might be a good time to let a monster eat him up! If this is a good time for the monster to eat up his peer, the child may be exhibiting what Smart and Smart (1972) referred to as *psychogenic theory*. This theory states that children can use play to help them resolve former experiences by assimilating new input into the old experience, thereby resolving conflicts. The new input would be the monster on the ship eating the peer up. The old experience would be whatever the peer did to the other youngster prior to the play context.

Certainly, play has many advantages for the preschooler, as he/she interacts with peers. Gaining control of situations and working through unresolved conflicts are just the beginning. And, in feeling empowered to act and react to pretend situations in ways that may be prohibited in real-life, the child can gain strength in his/her outlook on the events in life that may be uncomfortable for him/her. Take the following situation. When Mom turns the light out at bedtime, the youngster remembers that the monster ate his friend and is no longer hungry. Now the child can go to sleep. This may seem bizarre to adults, but it may be perfectly logical to the youngster. It can be seen by adults as a type of emotional crutch that youngsters might use to help gain internal security until a more mature understanding of invisible monsters is gained, along with acquiring other mechanisms for coping with stress. Most emotionally healthy children do grow out of the 'fear of the dark' or 'fear of a monster in the dark' syndrome with time.

Themes, Play, and Cognitive Development

Preschoolers have an enormous amount of fun playing in preschool. But how relevant is this fun in terms of laying the foundation for later academic achievement? Smart and Smart (1972) found that, "Engaging in this serious business, he develops his mind and body, integrating social and emotional functions and the intellectual functions of thinking, reasoning, problem solving, talking, and imaging" (p. 276). Berg (1994) said, "The degree of sophistication of a child's play was a better predictor of success in reading and writing in grade 1 than either IQ or socioeconomic level" (p. 37). Clearly, both Smart and Smart and Berg found that play adds to, enhances, and helps to develop the cognitive processes in the child, which are intellectual functions.

According to Dewey, constructive play is an integral part of the affective and communicative components of the child's success in later life. Roopnarine & Johnson (1993) said:

> Dewey's classroom was characterized by a hum of activity in which social negotiation and cooperation were among curriculum goals. . . . Constructive play and make-believe play were key elements of Dewey's curriculum. Coupled with the child's developing language and social skills, they formed the basis for both practical and aesthetic success. (p. 11).

Play seems to encompass all aspects of the young child's development. It helps the child to develop emotionally and socially. And play helps develop the intellect in terms of thinking, communicating, and problem solving, to name only a few components of the developmental process.

Thematic centers may offer a higher level of make-believe play in terms of children being interested in the theme as a focal point and *remaining in the play episode longer*. The longer period of interaction provides more opportunity for preschoolers to experience their peers' views. Mecca (1996) stated, "Children have to listen to each other and acknowledge what others are saying. . . ." (p. 73). This is thought to contribute to cognitive stimulation through the exchange of ideas, and adjustment to responses of peers. Youngsters are beginning to learn that other people's views can differ from theirs. The more time spent engaging in this exchange of ideas, the better.

Themes are generally presented on a broad scale so children are free to devise the directions they want their play episodes to take. For instance, with the broad theme 'gloves,' and many odd mittens and gloves displayed on a table, it would be interesting to see what type of play children would generate in preschool. This could be a good study. Perhaps the children would (a) pretend to sell gloves and mittens in a store, (b) decide to sort them by color or size, or (c) put gloves in a row and attempt to count them. These activities would be child-generated. Perhaps there would be some discrepancy among the youngsters as to what direction the play should take with the gloves. This could be called *disequilibrium* or *creative tension*.

Disequilibrium and creative tension are both terms that mean people do not agree with each other's point of view. These two phenomena can occur within the person, causing the person to think and rethink the circumstance in question. When youngsters are given more opportunity to experience disagreement, that is good because they must then negotiate terms for the play episode to continue with positive and progressive interaction. Youngsters must begin to use cognitive reasoning to gain understanding of each other's perspective. At this point children are just beginning to assimilate interactive communication, tolerance, acceptance, rejection, adaptation, and compromise into their social interaction. All of this social-living experience occurs in episodes of interactive play. Boyer (1997) suggested, "Qualities of playfulness are functions of a generally positive disposition that the child should possess . . . to adapt to her environment. Thus, playfulness serves as a constructive means for learning about the world" (p. 86).

Two Different Views of the Play Experience

Maria Montessori had a different view of play. According to Rogers and Sawyers (1988), Montessori didn't think that *just having fun* in the form of pretend play had much worth:

> Maria Montessori, for example, argued that pretend play was pathological, so she designed programs and materials to discourage such play in children. . . . The argument that play has no value for children appears to be based on the erroneous idea that play contributes little to adult behavior and development. (p. 55)

Montessori's program has, as its base, a more structured, specifically purposeful goal. The *goal-oriented* activities were children's work, according to Montessori. These activities had an aim and a purpose that the child was supposed to *achieve* before *moving on* to another work-activity. Montessori saw play as an unfocused and frivolous activity. She thought that ordered, organized, structured activities with objects (toys) that she designed offered the predictability and security that children needed in their lives. Her toys kept children focused and on target, according to Montessori. She did not seem to allow for the free flow of the children's imagination or creativity. Roopnarine and Johnson (1993) said, "Few free art materials are available in the traditional Montessori environment. When using art materials, children are encouraged to create in a goal-oriented way" (p. 253).

In response, Montessori proponents pointed out the following: (a) mastery of a task, due to error-free repetition of those tasks, (b) using the specialized materials that Montessori designed, and (c) lack of emphasis on social interaction while performing those specialized tasks are no cause for concern. Proponents said further, "joy comes from mastery, knowledge, achievement, and independence in the *real* work, not from role play" (p. 253). Montessori felt that a genuine intrinsic motivator for the children was the delight in accomplishing the work-activity itself. She believed that youngsters were motivated toward self-development and what she termed *auto-education* by working with Montessori materials. *Open-ended* play props had no place in her curriculum.

Open ended play props have potentially contributed to the more creative aspects of the preschooler's imagination. For example, given a large, empty box that a washing machine was delivered in, the preschooler has the choice of getting inside the box to become a bear in a cave, opening the other end of the box and crawling inside to become a car going through a tunnel, or getting inside the box and pretending it is a house in which to talk things over with an invisible friend. But when *something limiting* is added to the large box, the box can only be that specific thing. For instance, a large, empty washing machine box on which has been painted a door and a window, can only be a house. If someone paints four wheels on the box, it can only be a car or other motor vehicle. This may be one of the reasons that blocks are so popular. When playing with blocks a youngster can build anything he/she imagines, and the structure becomes real in the youngster's imagination, and thereby elicits play.

When preschoolers come together to play, they begin to learn to listen to the other person's point of view. Rogers and Sawyers (1988) called this learning experience *decentering*: "Children who engage in pretend play are able to decenter—to think about more than one viewpoint or thing at a time. This ability to decenter is inherent in many social skills as well. . . ." (p. 64). Wilburn (1997) stated, "Decentration refers to recognizing the other person's perspective as you plan your own action." Decentering and decentration are synonymous. These definitions suggest that youngsters are becoming acquainted with, and developing an appreciation for, other points of view which are in contrast to their own. Decentering represents a gradual relinquishing of egocentrism. It could also mean the group has acquiesced to a member's viewpoint, if that member can negotiate his/her viewpoint persuasively. In that case, the group will have decentered its point of view as it adopted the persuasive youngster's perspective.

In Summary

Play is an integral part of the preschool curriculum because of its benefits in the areas of language development, emotional and social development, intellectual development, and background for later academic development in general. Themes can enhance the play experience because youngsters may interact for longer periods of time. This would increase the opportunity to agree or disagree with each other, which could cause disequalibrium. Disequalibrium is uncomfortable. Therefore, children will negotiate terms of agreement, considering each other's perspectives in an effort to bring a balance, therefore a comfort, to the play scene. This is a higher cognitive process, which Piaget discussed.

Also in this chapter, Marie Montessori's views about the purposes of play were discussed, as well as the more traditional views of play as an expression of the child's coping mechanisms in times of stress, in times of creative expression, and in times of intellectual stimulation and social interaction. These are some of the issues that give us a well-rounded view of the preschooler and the activity called play. There is a need for further study in this most crucial area.

References

Berg, D. N. (1994). The role of play in literacy development. In P. Antonacci & C. N. Hedley (Eds.), *Natural approaches to reading and writing* (pp. 33–48). Norwood, NJ: Ablex Publishing.

Boyer, W. A. R. (1997). Enhancing playfulness with sensorial stimulation. *Journal of Research in Childhood Education, 12*(1), 78–87.

———— (1997). Playfulness enhancement through classroom intervention for the 21st century. *Childhood Education, 74*(2), 90–96.

Brewer, J. A., & Kieff, J. (1997). Fostering mutual respect for play at home and school. *Childhood Education, 73*(2), 92–96.

Cuffaro, H. K. (1974). Dramatic play—The experience of block building. In E. S. Hirsh (Ed.), *The block book* (pp. 69–88). National Association for the Education of Young Children, Washington, DC.

Gordon, A. M., & Browne, K. W. (1989). *Beginnings and beyond.* Albany, NY: Delmar Publishers.

Hartle, L. (1996). Effects of additional materials on preschool children's outdoor play behaviors. *Journal of Research in Childhood Education, 11*(1), 68–81.

Mecca, M. E. (1996). Classrooms where children learn to care. *Childhood Education, 73*(2), 72–74.

Rogers, C. S., & Sawyers, K. S. (1988). *Play in the lives of children.* National Association for the Education of Young Children, Washington, DC.

Roopnarine, J. L., & Johnson, J. E. (1993). *Approaches to early childhood education.* New York: Macmillan Publishing.

Smart, M. S., & Smart, R. C. (1972). *Children: Development and relationships.* New York: Macmillan Publishing.

Stone, S. J. (1996). Integrating play into the curriculum. *Childhood Education, 72*(2), 104–107.

Wallace, D. (1995). Nurturing the creative majority of our schools. *Childhood Education, 72*(1) 34–35.

Weller, M. A. (1996). *Play.* Compton's Interactive Encyclopedia, Softkey Multimedia Inc.

Wilburn, R. E. (1997). *Prosocial entry behaviors used by preschoolers to enter play groups in the natural setting of the classroom.* Published doctoral dissertation, Fordham University, New York.

Chapter 8

Scientific Inquiry—Naturally

The natural curiosity that is a fundamental part of a youngster lends itself easily to scientific inquiry. "Children may express curiosity about something and create a simple way to investigate it. . . . Children's curiosity is the place from which thinking and understanding emerge" (Church, 1997, p. 56). The quote implies that when youngsters are curious about something, they have the facility to create a *simple* way to find out more about what they are interested in. To illustrate, a child sees the two hands on the clock moving by themselves. He/she wants to open the clock and look inside to satisfy his/her curiosity as to how the hands move. It is a good thing that this particular clock is made to be opened and looked into. It is a teaching toy. There are many other interesting and informative topics to be found in the preschool environment, as we shall see.

Consider this preschool scene: "There's a spider in the bathroom! Come, come see it!" Within four seconds the small girls' lavatory was crowded with as many boys and girls as could physically fit into the space. "Where's the spider?" "Oohhh nnooo! Somebody pushed me and I stepped on it!" That scenario could be the beginning of a thematic unit on spiders, including the daily chapter reading of *Charlotte's Web*. Charlotte is a courageous spider who solves many problems on a farm. She is the best friend of Wilbur the pig, who gets into trouble a lot because he is so gullible.

Youngsters are full of curiosity, and their questions are part of their means of acquiring knowledge. "Questions like 'What do caterpillars eat?' can lead to a group exploration or a consultation with books about insects. Record children's further ideas and observations about caterpillars to compile a class caterpillar book" (Ross, 1995, p. 45). In fact, *insects* is a broad enough theme or topic as to allow preschoolers to delve into caterpillars, moths, butterflies, bugs, ants, and any number of other

available insects in spring and early summer. If some of the things men-
tioned are not technically insects, that fact will come out in the books and
discussions. Recording youngsters' increasing knowledge in any subject
can be accomplished by having them draw a representation of what they
have learned. This could be the beginning of a portfolio for later assessment.

The class may want to raise ladybugs. They take less than one month
to metamorphose from egg, to larva, to a skeletal stage. Then finally the
ladybug with red body and black dots arrives. It is now a full-fledged
beetle. Ladybugs can be purchased from garden centers or a group of
youngsters can pick them off the backs of leaves with the aid and guidance of an adult. This is one of those numerous occasions when class-
moms and class-dads can be very helpful for supervision. Some
preschoolers may not be ready to touch them. Some children, as well as
adults, are ready to *learn more about some things*, but are not ready to
physically interact with them. That's okay. No one should be forced to do
anything. After the children have investigated the insects, they can release the ladybugs back into nature.

Before collecting the bugs, a habitat has to be prepared to receive
them. A group of youngsters can do this preparation with a little guidance from the teacher. Preparing the habitat usually requires only a large
plastic container with a lot of small air holes on the top (or mesh wiring),
and some food for the bugs. A local pet-shop owner or a library book can
tell the teacher what food the bugs eat. Cohen (1994) suggested this,
"Watch a young child squatting intently over a pill bug as it inches across
a sidewalk . . . and you can see how completely captivating nature's
creatures can be" (p. 51).

Abundant language in the form of open dialogue will be forthcoming
as preschoolers observe the insects both outdoors on leaves and when
they are brought inside in plastic containers. Discussions and an exchange
of ideas concerning the insects are inevitable. "The cricket will eat the
food and we'll get him some more tomorrow." This is a hypothesis. Upon
arriving at preschool the next morning the child sees that some of the
food is still left in the plastic container, he/she then can adjust the hypothesis in view of the data. The observational data show that the cricket did
not eat all its food overnight. According to Goldhaber, these are *cognitively
challenging learning experiences* that are occurring in preschool.

Science is an intellectual pursuit that is both social and active. Children
should have time to play with scientific materials such as magnets, magni-
fying lenses, telescopes, tanks of water for sink/float and measuring activities, and tanks of sand for pouring and measuring. Combining water

and sand to make a kind of mud allows the child to be more in control of the outcome of his/her creation. The water will dampen the sand so that it does not spill so freely. "Playing with clay or mud allows children to control transformations more easily. Mud can be compressed into a ball, rolled out, then squeezed once more into a ball" (Segal & Adcock, 1986, p. 74). Mud is usually soil and water. But sand is more frequently found in the preschool classroom. Mud can be made in the play-yard by the children.

Preschoolers will tell anyone who listens what they are making in the sand bin, or what creation they have constructed out of clay. "Look what I made. It's a cake." "I made a snake." "I made a cake like Martha." "Let's put some more water on it." No, no! You'll make it too mushy!" Spitzley (1994) stated, "Language and science concepts expand as children learn about absorption, evaporation, and condensation, as well as properties of sand and water" (p. 38).

The attribute of malleability (ability to be reshaped many times) in clay and mud allows them to be manipulated and transformed into other shapes. This makes the two media attractive to youngsters. Children are learning that the form can be changed, but the ingredients or actual substance of the mixture remains the same. This knowledge is probably not on a conscious level, unless another person points it out to the child. Goldhaber (1994) said:

> Ideas are tested, discussed and made public. A learning environment that supports scientific inquiry must include materials that can be manipulated. . . . It must invite open and free dialogue so that ideas and hypotheses can be shared and challenged. . . . Resurgence of interest in science education provides . . . cognitively challenging learning experiences that characterize the play-based programs. (p. 26-27)

Most, if not all of the preschool curriculum is based on cognition through hands-on experiences, dialogue, and play.

Keeping Science Connected

Thematic units can offer an *integrated flow of connected components* that make up what this writer calls 'a continuing phenomenon.' This means that the ladybugs the children collected (science) can be discussed during circle time (language arts). This is a perfect time for the youngsters to tell about the time a personal situation happened to them involving a ladybug. "One time at the park a ladybug flew on my arm." Then the teacher can read a storybook with an insect connection and further discussion can follow (language arts). Class projects are generated in this way. The children can make up stories and drawings about the story they heard. Graphs and charts can be generated, which bring in the math component.

Thematic units can include hands-on initiation of a project, followed by discussion of what is being done, recording what is being observed, questioning what is being observed, answering those questions, and later, more discussion about the final product. After the insect investigation and observation has run its course, the topic could culminate in a group or class mural (art). This project would involve either all members of the class or a smaller group effort. It would be a visual, tangible, concrete result of the insect topic or theme. Topic, theme, and unit are used interchangeably in this chapter.

Songs, poems, and storybooks can be included in the unit, which lasts as long as the teacher and students are finding new areas to explore and investigate. Speaking of the teacher, Miller stated, "She decided to build on the children's interest by introducing experiences throughout the curriculum that enhanced this theme" (p. 42). Choices are to be decided between the teacher and the students, as often as possible. Jurek and MacDonald (1993) stated, "Offering experiences based on a theme the children chose, helped them learn about their world, organize information, and structure their thinking" (p. 31). There are preschools where a specific science curriculum is in place. The teacher has to adhere to the curriculum. However, as often as possible, the teacher and preschoolers will interject their own choices.

The outdoors is a great natural setting for discovery and exploration. When the *seasons begin and end*, natural displays of the elements exhibit the beginning and ending of *life's cycles*. Youngsters can take notice of this phenomenon and examine it. As school opens in September, the leaves are beginning to change colors. "Leaves were green all summer. Why are they changing to many colors at this time? Why are they falling off the trees? Let's gather some leaves for our classroom and discuss them" would be a good segue into a thematic unit on leaves, trees, bushes, and grass. The unit could be as broad as the children's curiosity allows.

Youngsters will begin to learn about the *discipline required for careful observation* of what they see. They can record findings, possibly in drawings and/or check-off charts. This could all be followed up by a class book of the observations in the form of drawings of each theme. "To be a good scientist, you need a whole set of skills, such as the ability to observe and record" (Cohen, 1997, p. 40). Miller said, "Using the scientific method, young scientists determine that screws rust in water, but plastic plates and wood don't" (p. 40).

When the snack is oranges, the preschoolers could be asked by their teacher to save all the seeds from their oranges. This is a natural procedure for beginning a thematic unit on seeds, planting seeds, observing sprouts, and observing the maturing plant. "Gardening is a good subject. You can grow your own food" (Cohen, p. 41). Even if you can only use a window-box planter, seed-growing can be exciting and informative for preschoolers as they water the seeds, and watch them sprout and grow. They can use string to graph the growth after the seeds sprout. All visual and concrete representations of the science topic help the youngster understand and internalize the process and the results.

Natural science is everywhere in the preschool environment as life cycles ebb and flow. Fresh grapes eventually turn into raisins, plums left to wither become prunes, and the orange seeds eventually push through the soil as their sprouts develop. This concrete, visual, hands-on natural science in preschool can have a spiraling effect as a theme is investigated on a basic, preschool level. The similar topics will be introduced and delved into more thoroughly in the elementary grades, and the children will have had a head-start. Beginning with basics is an *Ausubelian technique,* which means starting with the general, broad view of a topic, then narrowing the broad topic down to specifics for a finer, more in-depth investigation. Lawton (1993) offered, "Ausubel states that very young children must first learn 'primary concepts.' Preschool age children learn best in the presence of concrete examples of concepts that they can manipulate both physically and mentally . . ." (p. 158).

The basis for a love of scientific inquiry can begin here in preschool with young students learning to plant, water, observe, and record the progression of orange seeds. Much of the comparison, observation, and investigation in the preschool natural science corner can be self-directed in terms of the child having been previously shown how to use the materials and then they conduct the inquiry with minimum teacher guidance. Jurek and MacDonald (1993) suggested:

> Both the 4-year-old preschooler who compares her hand prints with her friend's and the 34-year-old biologist who compares various gene combinations in a lab share a basic human desire to find out how things work and to make sense of their world. This is the foundation of all scientific thinking. (p. 23)

Observation and comparison are basic skills that can be nurtured in preschool science and have far-reaching consequences. These two skills transfer over into math very easily whether the child is observing the sign in a math problem (plus or minus) in elementary grades, or observing how tall the plant has grown this week in preschool. The observation and comparison skills could potentially be sharper for a student in later grades due to the student having begun those skills in preschool.

When leaves and rocks are collected, students observe differences and compare similarities such as color, shape, size, and stratified layers of sediment in rocks. Observation, comparison, and discussion can open the way for questions and recording results. This approach is interdisciplinary, meaning it can cross the domains of language arts, scientific inquiry, math, and art. This encompasses the "whole-child" learning mode. The concepts are continuing phenomena.

Methods of Recording Observations

It is important to remember that in preschool some of the methods of *recording observations and results* are captured in drawings, cut-and-paste graphs, and pasting pieces of colored felt to the bottom of the drawings to represent the plant or whatever the scientific inquiry is about. Preschoolers can further record their observations and results by dictating to teachers what they have observed. Rosen (1994) stated, "Be sure children can do something active with the objects in all your displays. That might mean weighing them, making rubbings, or simply looking at them through a magnifier" (p. 59). Simply having a 'don't touch' display that is beautiful to observe, but cannot be handled, is never appropriate for preschool.

By providing preschoolers with some materials and having them gather natural objects from the yard or on a walk around the school, the early childhood teacher fosters the process of scientific inquiry in a natural progression. Stone and Glascott (1997) stated:

> Opportunities for free-play with science materials promote a child's curiosity and willingness to consider varying options. Children will make their own discoveries during free play with their chosen science materials and they will construct their own knowledge of a phenomenon. Through choice, children feel ownership of the process. (p. 103)

Youngsters will usually find a way to 'play' with materials when they are made available to them. They will "find ways to explore and create their own activities. . . . A group of magnets and materials left on a science table after a discussion and demonstration will inspire children to make discoveries with their peers" (Leipzig, 1994, p. 68).

In Summary

Scientific inquiry can be naturally and comfortably included in the preschool curriculum by using activities that mark the recurring seasons and the life and death cycles in natural phenomena. That phenomena includes leaves turning from green to brown and falling from the trees, by observing pumpkins turning from round to withered caved-in specimens, and more.

Questions and the discovery of some answers can create a desire to know more about natural science at this early age. If the love of science is begun in the early years, it will usually continue into the later school career of most children. Cohen (1997) said, "We have good evidence that the best way to get children to do well in science later is to approach science developmentally early on" (p. 41).

Classroom use of storybooks, songs, poems, original stories, and drawings to present a theme in science may further enhance the enthusiasm for the topic. This helps give a holistic approach to the subject matter. For example, youngsters can begin to see the connections between what they are learning in the science area and the pictures and words in some of their favorite books and songs. "The itsy, bitsy spider goes up the water spout. Down comes the rain to wash the spider out. Out comes the sun to dry up all the rain. But the itsy, bitsy spider goes up the spout again." The song about a spider connects science with language and music (rhythm).

In this popular preschool song, the youngsters can begin to make a connection between water and rain, and between the sun and its ability to dry things out. These facts are obvious to adults, but how and when did we first learn these facts, and what helped us make connections between them and our lives? Anyway, why did the spider go back up the waterspout? And, what is a spout? These are clarifying questions that should be explored in preschool science. The children can even make up a spider or butterfly dance to go along with the theme. Anything kinesthetic would be welcomed. The success of a preschool science curriculum rests on including what the children are interested in. Children can learn to enjoy science in preschool with successful consequences well into their later school years.

References

Church, E. B. (1997). Are those really diamonds? *Early Childhood Today, 11*(80), 56–57.

Cohen, R. (1997). Teaching science to young children. *Early Childhood Today, 11*(8), 40–41.

Jurek, D., & MacDonald, S. (1993). Exploring living things. *Pre-K Today, 7*(6), 22–31.

Goldhaber, J. (1994). If we call it science, then can we let the children play? *Childhood Education, 71*(1), 24–27.

Lawton, J. T. (1993). The ausubelian preschool classroom. In J. L. Roopnarine, & J. E. Johnson (Eds.), *Approaches to early childhood* (pp. 157–177). New York: Macmillan Publishing Co.

Leipzig, J. (1994). Cooperative learning: Creating a classroom community. *Early Childhood Today, 9*(1), 62–69.

Miller, S. A. (1994). Sand and water around the room. *Early Childhood Today, 8*(6), 37–41.

Rosen, I. (1994). Setting up a super science center. *Early Childhood Today, 9*(7), 58–59.

Ross, M. E. (1995). Investigating nature. *Early Childhood Today, 9*(8), 40–47.

Segal, M., & Adcock, D. (1986). *Your child at play: Three to five years.* New York: Newmarket Press.

Stone, S. L., & Glascott, K. (1997). The affective side of science instruction. *Childhood Education, 74*(2), 102–104.

Chapter 9

Young Artists

Young children enjoy expressing themselves verbally, kinetically, and creatively through art. Verbally means "communicating through speaking," as used in this chapter. Kinetically means "through movement, physically active." Children enjoy talking to peers and adults about whatever is currently of interest to them. Even a shy child will usually begin to converse if something that he/she is interested in is being discussed. Children will run, jump, roll, skip, and do anything else that is active when the space allows. They also like to express themselves through their creations.

Youngsters enjoy creating structures with blocks, objects with clay, drawings with crayons and paper, and collages with a hodgepodge of recyclable materials. Then they talk about these creations to communicate their emotions, thereby building self-esteem.

Stages in Early Art

Smart and Smart (1972) offered a series of maturational stages that can be identified as youngsters progress in creating their art pieces. *Scribbling stage* is said to be from 1-to-3-years-of-age. In this stage children will make marks on paper, in sand, on the sidewalk, on the wall, almost anywhere. Youngsters use different types of strokes in this stage. The strokes are usually more straight than curved, and more long than short. When using paints and paintbrushes, there tends to be a back and forth motion that is applied with pressure. This pressure could result in the paper getting holes in it.

In the next stage, called *shape and design*, youngsters are between 2-and-5-years-old. Creations in this stage are conglomerates of lines and curves learned in the scribbling stage. Usually these creations are done for pleasure and not to represent anything in particular. However, for *some* preschoolers their creations *do* represent something specific.

In the last stage, children are 4-years-old and older. It is called the *pictorial* stage, where youngsters use lines, curves, shapes, and designs to represent what they perceive as *reality*. "All over the world, children make their early drawings in the same ways. Their pictures of people, houses, trees, suns, boats, trains, and cars give little hint as to whether the young artists were American, Scottish, or Indonesian" (Smart & Smart, 1972, p. 292).

It would seem that cultural input would have some influence on the way houses looked and the clothes that people wore in children's drawings from different parts of the world. However, Smart and Smart said in the quote that children "make their early drawings in the same ways." Perhaps the quote refers to the general use of basic lines, curves, shapes, and general designs that represent reality to the children. It would seem that anything specific would be influenced by culture. But then early drawings created by youngsters don't usually have much detail. This would be a good study to conduct today.

Emotions in Art

Look at the colors youngsters select when there is an array of many crayons, markers, and paints. Look at the wide sweeps of the brush or the small sweeps of the marker. Does this tell you anything about how the child is feeling and expressing those feelings? Feinburg (1993) stated:

> One of the most powerful things about creating art is that it allows artists to express emotion. This is particularly important for young children because it is often easier for them to communicate feelings through art than through words. . . . And at the same time that the process of art allows children to express their feelings, the products they create let them share their expressions with others. (p. 58)

When preschoolers are exuberant, their art may be quite different in terms of shape, color, shading, and even content than when they are melancholy. Mood has an influence on what a person wants to portray in his/her creations. Very possibly the preschooler who is melancholy won't even paint or play with the clay because he/she might prefer to sulk and cry. Sulking and crying are ways of getting the adult's attention.

Young children want the adults in their lives to know when they are unhappy. They want adults to change the situation. This writer witnessed the following episode in a preschool classroom: "Don't you see I'm cryin'?" screamed a girl about 4-years-old. "Yes, I do," replied the teacher. "What are you gonna [*sic*] do about it? I want that bike!" The teacher's response was, "I'm going to talk to Marc while you sit there and wait your turn to ride the bike, or you can play with something else. And you can keep crying if you choose to." The girl did keep crying for a short time. She stopped when she was ready; and, she rode the bike when it was her turn to do so.

When youngsters use media like clay, mud, sand, and paper and paints, creations in these media can offer a time snapshot in which to capture the child's mood. This can be therapeutic for a child. If a child did color, paint, draw, or make something with clay while upset, it would be interesting to save that art and compare it to art the same youngster created on a happy, exuberant day. There is bound to be a difference in mood, colors, lines, curves, and general appearance. It would be an interesting informal experiment.

When other people can appreciate one's creations, a sense of enhanced self-esteem is usually the result. A shy child can gain recognition and feel empowered through the process of creating art. The young student might be encouraged to exhibit his/her art during Show-and-Tell and discuss the art piece with peers.

The creation process can be a 'developing process' of the particular art piece until its completion. The term *developing process* refers to an activity that is not completed on the day it is begun. Generally speaking, preschoolers like to see closure of a project by the end of the day. However, if more steps are needed to complete the art project, the child should be told in advance that the process leading to completion needs to be continued the next day. For example, if a piece of clay sculpture needs to dry overnight, and then be sprayed the next day so that it becomes more durable, the preschooler will have to wait a day or two before delivering it to Mom and Dad. This 2-day process should be explained to the child before the art project is begun. Preschoolers do not usually like to have gratification delayed. They are in the egocentric stage of development, according to Piaget, and delayed gratification is not one of their strong points.

The Art Creating Process

Creating something is a way of giving 'life' to the thing. That is a very powerful emotion. "Children can look at their work and think, 'I made this; this was from my idea.' When children feel they are competent creators, a sense of personal power develops" (Feinburg, p. 60). Ask an author, sculptor, painter, or anyone who creates something that has permanency, and that person will testify to the feeling of having "given life" to his/her creation. Ownership comes with the creating process and product. Adults must be very careful to respect the children's creations.

In order for the *art creating process* to be uninhibited, many items and materials should be available to the youngsters, so that they feel free to select the different media they want to express themselves through. Referring to preschoolers, Miller (1996) said, "They learn to discriminate among shapes, colors, textures, and sizes as they select different materials—lace, cork, feathers, and more—to use in this open-ended activity" (p. 15). Lots of colors, textures, shapes, types of paper, and other artistic materials should be placed within easy reach. Materials on low shelves and in accessible cabinets and cubbies will help to ensure the feeling in the child that it is okay to use these materials. "I can get what I need," is the feeling that such a classroom fosters in a youngster. "Your role as a patron of children's art is to supply space to work plus interesting materials" (Kristeller, 1995, p. 36).

Time span is another important consideration in the art curriculum. It should be long enough to allow for thought and conversation, revisions and re-creations. Sometimes creating art may be a solitary event where the youngster prefers to be alone to mold the clay or paint the picture. At other times the artist will enjoy the companionship of peers who may be engaged in creating their own art. This is a situation where artistic vocabulary would be used as the conversation flowed. "I'm painting the grass green. Then I'm gonna [sic] paste brown string on it for the worms." "Look, I put my ladybug on the grass. But it look big [sic], huh? I'ma [sic] just put some brown string too." These quotes are excerpts from a conversation between peers in a preschool classroom. This is 'art language' in which vocabulary and cognition are expanded to process ideas that may not have occurred ordinarily as the youngsters engaged in 'regular' play.

Cognitively, it may take planning and structuring of thoughts as some youngsters create a piece of artwork. "Do children seem to know ahead of time what they want to create?" (Kristeller, p. 36). Some children will just smear the paste and the paper and begin to put pieces of felt, crepe paper, buttons, and other things together. These youngsters appear to be discovering what will turn up as they spontaneously design their art. "Are they using the materials for self-expression (intrapersonal) or for exploration of properties (logical/mathematical)" Kristeller, p. 36, words in parenthesis by this writer. It seems to be this early process of discovery that brings about the later planning and structuring in some children's future creations. The child who begins to create with plan and structure may be the innate gifted artist. Brodkin (1996) offered:

> He selected some markers and paper and then slid into a familiar chair. As always, it was fascinating to watch him work. Most fours don't do representative drawings at all, yet his have details such as 'Grandma's hair' and 'the blue flowers on her dress'. . . . Often when he's drawing, he doesn't notice the other children around him. . . . I know what's on his mind because he talks about the drawings. (p. 9)

It would be interesting to follow up on this youngster and others like him who exhibited artistic ability in their early years in preschool. All children are capable of producing art, to varying degrees; but some children are gifted. Both types of artistic processes are exhibited in preschool: (a) smear and paste, and (b) plan and structure. "As children experiment and investigate, they learn about the physical nature of tools and material. What will the brush do if I hit it on the paper this way . . ." (Feinburg, p. 60). This is a thoughtful consideration of the artistic process, which needs ample time to flourish. "The child needs optimum freedom to mold materials, to create puppet characters. The child also needs time and space to bring the character to dramatic life" (Polito, 1994, p. 56). Bringing the puppet character to dramatic life is an extension of creation that naturally flows into sharing the creation during Show-and-Tell. Language flows, ideas flow, and self-esteem is enhanced during this display of art.

Using Integrative Skills

While developing investigation and experimentation skills in art, the youngster is also refining some of the same skills that are needed for science and mathematics, to be used later in his/her school career. Similar cognitive processes are used for art as are used for later academics. For instance, the *wide sweeps* and *circular motions* of the paintbrush and marker that the preschooler uses in art are *spatial movements* and *geometric shapes and curves*. The preschooler will use these concepts and movements later in math. The movements are now rudimentary, but they are still spatial and geometric none the less.

Feinburg (1993) said the "large sun form with extending legs and arms that preschoolers create to represent people" (p. 60) is usually the most familiar objective or representative art in preschool. When the teacher gives the youngster a blank sheet of paper, the teacher is asking for the child to create art. The child may produce the "large sun form with

extending legs and arms" that Feinburg spoke about, or something similar. But whatever the child produces is his/her art creation. The youngster may or may not name it. Adults should not insist on a name for art in
preschool or at home because the child may not be at the developmental
stage where naming is important to him/her. Or, maybe it has not yet
occurred to the child that what he/she is creating has to represent anything except the exploration and fun that using the materials offer to
him/her personally.

When the teacher gives the child a sheet of paper with an apple on it
to color, the teacher is asking the child to color an apple. This is *not*
creating art. Kristeller said, "By definition, art is open-ended, with the
artist determining the form the work will take" (p. 36). The difference is
obvious because the original emotions and original creations of the child
will be forthcoming on the blank sheet of paper. There is a time and place
for both of these activities in preschool. But educators and other adults
must recognize the difference when planning an *art curriculum*. The
youngster has to create the entire design for it to be called his/her art.

In Summary

The preschool classroom needs to have an active art curriculum. The art
curriculum needs to be a daily part of the routine, with ample time for
youngsters to explore the art materials and give due consideration to the
social component of creating and then sharing the creations with each
other. Keep in mind that some children may prefer to create their art
quietly and alone. Being solitary while creating is okay.

Smart and Smart (1972) indicated stages that preschoolers progress
through as they mature from using crayons and markers to drawing re-
productions of reality, as they see it. Accordingly, the stages progress
from scribbling, to shape and design, to the third and final pictorial stage,
which represents reality, as the child perceives it. Children all over the
world are said to spend at least some time in these three stages of art
development. Further, children from all over the world are said to produce
similar 'stage one' art, *scribbling stage* (Smart & Smart).

In the progression from the discovery and exploratory stages of the art
materials, to the consummate piece of art that youngsters create, it seems
to be the *process* as well as the product that brings satisfaction to the
young artists. The conversations, the sharing of ideas while the work is in
progress, and then presentation of the art work itself, perhaps at Show-
and-Tell, are all vital pieces of the art curriculum in preschool.

References

Brodkin, A. M. (1996). Why is Albert always in the art corner? *Early Childhood Today, 10*(4), 9, 11.

Feinburg, W. G. (1993). Learning through art. *Early Childhood Today, 8*(2), 58-63.

Kristeller, J. (1995). A classroom for every child. *Early Childhood Today, 10*(1), 35–40.

Miller, S. A. (1996). Look what I did! *Early Childhood Today, 10*(4), 15, 17.

Polito, T. (1994). How play and work are organized in a kindergarten classroom. *Journal of Research, 9*(1), 47–57.

Smart, M. S., & Smart, R. C. (1972). *Children: Development and relationships.* New York: Macmillan Publishers

Chapter 10

Amazing Math

Like science, it seems that math is everywhere in the preschool classroom. The child crawls *inside* the large box and comes *outside* again. He/she goes *up* the sliding board to the *top*, and propels *down* again to the *bottom*. Or the child may sit in the *middle* of the sliding board and observe the surroundings in the play-yard. Inside, outside, up, down, top, bottom, and middle are math concepts. Children can actually and concretely perform these math directional concepts. They can manipulate objects to place them in the position the direction states, or they can put *themselves* (position their own bodies) in these positions. When the youngster places one spoon next to each teacup in the housekeeping area, he/she knows that everyone in the housekeeping area will have make-believe tea. When that same youngster gives every child a cookie and three cookies are left over, how can he/she distribute them equally? That's a math dilemma. This dilemma will be discussed later in this chapter.

Preschool youngsters are concrete in their ability to perceive math concepts. This means they need to touch objects and visualize the concepts being discussed. Mental imagery is very important to their understanding a concept. If youngsters can see it and physically manipulate materials, they stand a better chance of *beginning to understand* the concept. They need to work through each concept one step at a time. For example, when there are three shoes in a pile belonging to two friends, one preschooler will realize his/her shoe is missing when his peer takes his/her pair of shoes from the pile to put them on, and there is only one shoe remaining. That youngster will then say, "Hey, where's my other shoe?" because he/she has to have the experience of visualizing the missing shoe.

When snack is being prepared, the helper realizes that all the children at 'table one' will have snack because he/she puts a napkin in front of each chair. Then the second helper puts the cookie on each napkin. Next, the third helper puts a juice box next to each cookie. The one-to-one correspondence is a hands-on experience that relates to the preschooler that everyone will have snack. If he/she runs out of juice boxes before every cookie has a juice box next to it, the helper will point and say, "I need a juice for this cookie." He/she may not have learned that if he/she had counted the cookies and then counted the juices, and came up short a juice, he/she would have known in advance that another juice was needed. The counting, without tactile substance, is just a rhythmic chant, so to speak, at preschool level.

The Snack—An Informal Experiment

Interesting elements come to the fore when the teacher says, "We have four chairs at table one, and each chair has a snack in front of it. But we have two cookies left over. How can we share these cookies with every one at 'table one?' An informal experiment was conducted in a preschool classroom with 11 youngsters. These children were between 4-and-5-years-old. They attended an all-day program. Six were boys and five were girls. The experiment was informal in terms of it not being conducted again for validity, and no variables were considered. The preschoolers were selected randomly, though.

Procedure of the Snack Experiment

Each of the 11 preschool students was taken into the room next door, one preschooler at a time. Only two people were in the room at any one time, the preschooler and the interviewer. Four chairs were placed at a table. In front of each chair the interviewer had already set up a napkin with one cookie on it. As each preschooler walked in, the interviewer said, "Each chair has a snack in front of it. Soon four children will come and sit down to eat their snack. Let's count the snacks to see if there are four snacks, one, two, three, four."

As the interviewer counted from one to four, she touched each napkin, as a visual effect for the preschooler. Then she told the preschooler to count again and touch each napkin, just the way the interviewer had done. "How many children will have snack?" asked the interviewer. Each of the 11 preschoolers answered that four children would have a snack. The interviewer then continued, "Our problem is this—we have two cookies left over. How can we share these *two* cookies with all *four* children?" As the interviewer said, "all four children," she pointed to each chair. She then gave the two cookies to the preschooler and said, "Think about how to share these two cookies with all *four* students so that everyone will be happy."

Results of the Snack Experiment

Boys. Of the six boys, three did the same thing. They put a whole cookie down on each of two napkins, looked up at the interviewer to signal completion of the task. One of the three said, "I shared." Another child asked, "Like this?" The interviewer made the same reply to each of the children in their turn, "These two children will be happy because they have two whole cookies. But these two children will be sad because they still have only one cookie. Can you think of a way to share the two extra cookies with all four people?" These preschoolers spent some time moving the two extra cookies back and forth between the four snacks, never even considering breaking each cookie in half, or at least in pieces, to place one piece of the broken cookie on each of the four napkins.

The fourth boy just stood next to one of the four chairs. He stood holding the two extra cookies, after the interviewer explained the problem. The interviewer explained the situation a second time to him because he didn't move after the first explanation. He just continued to stand there. This boy was then taken back to his class. He was very familiar with the interviewer, and did not visibly display any anxiety while with the interviewer. He was with her daily for the past two years. The only explanation the interviewer can offer for his behavior is that the boy either felt overwhelmed because he could not think of what to do with the extra cookies, or he just wanted to go back to his preschool classroom, to play. He did previously say that he wanted to go into the room next door to help the interviewer with a problem, so he was not forced into the situation.

The fifth and sixth boys thought of the solution immediately. One said while looking towards the interviewer, "We could break the cookies." The interviewer nodded consent. He broke the two cookies in half and placed one piece on each of the four napkins. The cookies were graham crackers, so they broke evenly along perforated lines. After he was taken back to his classroom, the sixth preschooler just broke the cookies in half and placed one piece on each napkin, without first making the statement of what he was going to do.

Girls. Of the five girls, three did not solve the problem. They did exactly what the three boys had done, who had not solved the problem. The three girls just placed a whole cookie on two of the four napkins. They spent some time looking at the cookies, placing them first on this napkin, then on that napkin, then looking at the interviewer for a response. Each time they looked up at the interviewer, they were asked to think of another way to share the two cookies with all four children. It's important to remember that only one youngster was in the room with the interviewer at a time. Each child was taken back to the classroom after a turn with the interviewer. The last two girls *did* solve the problem. They both said right away to break the cookies and share them. The interviewer asked each girl how she was going to share the cookies. Each girl just put a piece of cookie on the four napkins Miller. (1998) said, "Preschoolers are mastering one-to-one correspondence and the concept of numbers. But they're still in the preoperational phase and are more concrete than logical. Threes and fours tend to base their judgments on how things look." (p. 14). This is concurrent with Piaget and Inhelder (1969).

This informal experiment helps us to understand that preschoolers are concrete and visual, which according to Piaget means 'preoperational.' Children at the preschool age are not able to think abstractly. They do much better touching, smelling, tasting, hearing, and seeing as they learn, using all or as many senses as possible at one time.

The Beads—A Second Informal Experiment

Another activity in preschool is sorting objects into groups by a particular characteristic or attribute. Generally speaking, a few preschool youngsters may begin to sort by one attribute or characterization of an object. An informal experiment was conducted in which thirteen preschoolers were given a bucket full of multi-colored, large, wooden beads with various shapes. Some beads were shaped like spools, some were square, some were rather oval, and some were oval with grooves cut in the sides.

Procedure of the Beads Experiment

Each preschooler was given a bucket of beads and an empty gray tray that had four compartments in it. The students were called to a table one at a time to play with the materials so that no child would be influenced to use the materials in the same way that a peer was using them. Each student was told he/she could play with the beads by making groups of beads to put into the tray slots. Nothing else was said by way of instruction. Some students asked, "What you [sic] want me to do?" The interviewer answered, "You can play with the beads and the tray by making groups or piles of beads." This answer was intentionally vague.

Four of the youngsters were girls, and nine were boys, for a total of 13 participants. They were enrolled in a full-day preschool program. The students were all between 4- and 5-years-old. Because of the year's span of age difference, this informal experiment is not offered as a means of comparison of youngsters' abilities. It is offered to show that there may be varying ages and abilities in the preschool classroom. Therefore, the teacher cannot have one set of expectations for the entire class of preschoolers.

Results of the Beads Experiment

Boys. Five of the nine boys took the beads by the handful and placed them into the four compartments of the tray. These boys were not concerned about the shape or color of the beads. The boys just scooped the beads up by the handful and deposited them in the four compartments. Then they said they were finished. When they were finished playing with the beads, each child left the table to play with peers in another part of the classroom. Remember, these students sat at different times to play with the materials. So they were not influenced by each other. The sixth boy just piled the beads into the tray and was not mindful that the beads were not evenly distributed into each compartment of the tray. He just dumped a handful of beads onto the top of the tray, and the beads fell where they may. He then sat there until the interviewer asked him if he wanted to play with the beads anymore. He replied, "No," and left the table to join his peers.

The seventh boy studied each bead that he picked up for a short time (about 4 seconds), then he placed it down in a compartment of the tray. He sometimes put one bead to another, end-to-end in the air, not on the table and observed the two beads. But he did not attempt to actually make a tower by placing the two beads on the table. He remained engaged for about three minutes. The boy seemed to be observing the different shapes of the beads. He looked through the hole that ran through the middle of the bead. He remained engaged for about 4 minutes. This child handled about 20 beads during the 4 minutes. He was not rushed and seemed to be methodical in his observation and handling of the beads and placing each one in a compartment. He did not seem to have a discernible reason for placing each bead in a particular tray compartment because there were many colors and shapes in each compartment. It appeared that he put one bead in the first compartment, the next bead in the next compartment, the third bead in the third compartment, and so on.

The eighth boy emptied the beads onto the floor. Then he sorted them by *green* color. He ignored all other colors. After the *green activity*, he then tried to build a structure using all the beads, green included. He called to no one in particular, "I'm building a house." He lost interest after about 3 minutes. During the three minutes, he attempted to build a flat house, then a tall house. He talked to himself in a voice too low for this writer to hear what he was saying. But, it appeared that he was in a conference with himself about his activity with the beads.

The ninth boy picked up the bucket and poured the beads into the four compartments of the tray. He then tried to pour the beads back into the bucket from the tray. Some of the beads fell all around the bucket. He picked them up one by one and put them in the bucket and left. It took him about 90 seconds to do all this.

Girls. Two of the four girls put the beads by the handful into each compartment of the tray. They did not seem to care about color or shape, just that each compartment had beads in it. When all the beads were out of the bucket and into each compartment of the tray, they left the table. This was done one girl at a time; they did not influence each other.

The third girl poured the beads indiscriminately into each compartment of the tray by turning the bucket upside down. She then diligently worked with the beads by picking out red beads to form a long train-like structure on the table. Later she put other colors on the structure so that the first part of the train was red and the latter part was multicolored. She worked with the beads for about seven minutes. She left abruptly without apparent reason.

The last girl put beads in the tray compartments by the handful. Then she thoughtfully built an orange tower using only one particular shape, so that her tower was uniform in color and shape. This preschooler used *two* attributes of the beads, *shape and color*. This was not done by any other preschooler. She remained about four minutes, adding on to the structure, then removing beads and adding on again. It was not clear why she removed some beads and put more on because the added beads were the kind that she had removed. When she was satisfied with the structure, she left the table.

This informal experiment is offered to show that some preschoolers can spend time attempting to figure out details when they are interested in the task. Also of interest is the varied types of activities that the preschoolers exhibited. Some children appeared to be happy just handling the beads and moving them from the bucket into the compartments of the tray. Others used certain attributes of the beads as criteria for their activity.

At the preschool level, numbers are not meaningful unless there are concrete objects to match with the numbers. To illustrate, "When 4-year-old Josh picks up the Lincoln Logs and finishes counting, '1, 2, 3, 4,' he knows that he is holding four logs" (Miller, 1998, p. 15). This is one-to-one correspondence on a meaningful level in preschool. Youngsters come to realize that the last number they say *is the number of objects in their pile* after touching and counting the objects over a period time. Because youngsters are using touch and sight to help them cognitively internalize the concept of number, the concept becomes reality for them through their senses and intellect working together.

In preschool, when youngsters learn to recognize the four basic shapes—circle, square, rectangle, and triangle—they are learning a rudiment of geometry. The children are learning spatial skills in terms of visually recognizing the configuration these shapes take and where the shapes can possibly fit. Colors are usually taught in connection with shapes and objects that they can touch. For example, a red square bead or block and a blue circular bead have more meaning to the youngster than just the two-dimensional shape of a red square and a blue circle on a sheet of paper.

In Summary

In summary, because math is embedded all around the environment in preschool, it is easy and natural to incorporate it into daily activities. It is natural for a preschool teacher to say, "We have yellow bananas for snack today," or "red apples," or "green grapes." Doors and windows have a rectangular shape. Buttons have a circular shape. These shapes can be made reference to in most conversations and at teachable moments.

'Teachable moments' are those times when the situation or conversation naturally leads to an explanation of a circumstance. For instance, "Mary won't share the doll, teacher." Yoli said this with much frustration because she knew that sharing was one of the class rules that the children and teacher had established. However, it was now clear that Yoli needed further explanation of what 'sharing' really means in the classroom setting. The teacher asked Yoli if Mary had the doll first. "Yes, but now I want it," said Yoli. The teacher told Yoli that she had to wait until Mary finished playing with the doll, or that Yoli could get the other doll to play with if she didn't want to wait. "Mary keeps the doll she has now because she got the doll first. Sharing means giving one doll to you, Yoli, if Mary had two dolls. It does not mean that Mary has to give up the doll to you, just because you want it and you say so." Needless to say, that teachable moment did not go over big with Yoli, but Mary liked it just fine.

Youngsters are learning math concepts in preschool just by being in the classroom and conversing with peers, aides, and the teacher. They talk about the different attributes of objects, the hands-on fun experiences with manipulatives, the play-yard experiences of going in and out of large boxes, going up and down the slide, and being on top, in the middle, and on the bottom of the climbing bars. It would be difficult to experience a day in preschool that had no reference to a math concept!

References

Miller, S. A. (1998). The path to math. *Early Childhood Today, 12*(4), 14–15.

Piaget, J., & Inhelder, B. (1969). *The psychology of the child*. New York: Basic Books.

Chapter 11

Philosophical Summary

Children *can* learn when they are given time to internalize new material. This internalization process is an "overt act on the part of the learner to assimilate data from the environment" according to Piaget (Marek, 1992, p. 266). Interactive experiences with other children in a stimulating environment encourage *assimilation* of new material with what the children already know.

The more patience and encouragement adults offer children, the more children are convinced they can achieve anything. "I can do it. Let me do that." These words are heard where children learn by 'doing' rather than just by listening to lectures. This means that a youngster interacts with the environment and all it contains. The child is a constructivist learner, according to Bologna (1995) which means he/she explores the environment, and uses what he/she finds to help make meaning out of his surroundings. He/she attempts to sort through the information and activities, putting them into mental categories. In doing this, the child helps to construct meaning for himself/herself. In this process, the child may experience confusion, disequilibrium.

Confusion and disequilibrium mean a full understanding of the information has not yet taken place within the youngster. The child then recalls some things he/she already knows and uses them to help him/her understand the new information. This is termed accommodation of new information. For example, all animals with four legs are called 'doggies' by a child until he/she learns that only the four-legged animals that bark are actually doggies Piaget & Inhelder , 1969). Assimilation of new information occurs when a child begins to understand that doggies, kitties, horses, squirrels, etc., are all termed animals because they occupy an existence of living things that we don't call *humans* or *people*. The child assembles for himself/herself the new information (concept) *animal* into what he/she already knows about living things. Accommodation and assimilation do have similarities. But they are not really interchangeable concepts.

Construction of learning based on individual experiences, both actual and imagined, should be the foundation of any program for students, but especially for you students. Vygotsky said that youngsters first interact socially (and learning is a social endeavor), then later they think over what they did while interacting socially. This process of thinking and sorting through the day's events helps the young child to construct what meaning the events has for him/her. The process of reflection is crucial, after the 'doing' has occurred (reflection and thinking and sorting are used here as interchangeable mental activities).

Embedded in this reflective thinking and sorting are visual images that youngsters can use "as tools to help them sort out, understand, and cope with their environment" (Hubbard, p. 104) in their efforts to construct meaning for themselves. Mental imagery is another crucial process that can help to solidify experiences in a person's memory, regardless of the person's age. The 'hands-on, doing' approach to teaching and learning would seem to enable mental imagery to occur.

Enrolling a child in preschool or a play group around the age of three offers countless opportunities for social interactive experiences, as well as an introduction to routine and schedule that is different from the home. The realization that other people do not necessarily do everything the way 'Mommy and Daddy' does it is an introduction into the wider society. This is an aid in the process of socializing the child into our multicultural society. Certainly a large portion of interactive experiences, conversations, routines, and other socially cultural activities have been already introduced to the preschooler before he/she has entered preschool. However, learning more of these activities in an environment outside of the home is good start as an introduction into society.

References

Bologna, T. A. (1995). Integration of the abilities that foster emerging literacy. In C. N. Hedley, P. Antonacci, & M. Rabinowitz (Eds.), *Thinking and literacy* (pp. 153–165). Hillsdale, NJ: Lawrence Erlbaum Publishers.

Hubbard, R. (1992). Images: partners with words for making meaning. In C. Hedley, D. Feldman, and P. Antonacci (Eds.), *Literacy across the curriculum* (pp. 87–116). Norwood, NJ: Ablex Publishing.

Marek, E. A. (1992). Conceptualizing in science: misconception research using a constructivist model. In C. Hedley, D. Feldman, and P. Antonacci (Eds.), *Literacy across the curriculum* (pp. 266–285). Norwood, NJ: Ablex Publishing.

Piaget, J., & Inhelder, B. (1969). *The psychology of the child.* New York: Basic Books.

References

Index

RETHINKING CHILDHOOD

JOE L. KINCHELOE & JANICE A. JIPSON, *General Editors*

A revolution is occurring regarding the study of childhood. Traditional notions of child development are under attack, as are the methods by which children are studied. At the same time, the nature of childhood itself is changing as children gain access to information once reserved for adults only. Technological innovations, media, and electronic information have narrowed the distinction between adults and children, forcing educators to rethink the world of schooling in this new context.

This series of textbooks and monographs encourages scholarship in all of these areas, eliciting critical investigations in developmental psychology, early childhood education, multicultural education, and cultural studies of childhood.

Proposals and manuscripts may be sent to the general editors:

Joe L. Kincheloe
637 W. Foster Avenue
State College, PA 16801

or

Janice A. Jipson
219 Pease Court
Janesville, WI 53545

To order other books in this series, please contact our Customer Service Department at:

(800) 770-LANG (within the U.S.)
(212) 647-7706 (outside the U.S.)
(212) 647-7707 FAX

Or browse online by series at:
www.peterlang.com